We Have Something To Say:
True Stories From Adolescent Girls Growing Up In The Slums Of Kampala

Created by Megan Walrod, in partnership with Girl Up Initiative Uganda

Taylor~
may these girls + their
stories inspire you as they do me!
And - what else is possible when
we follow our knowing + allow
it to create more for more people?!
♡ Megan

12·7·2020

Cover design by Walusimbi Emmanuel and Connie Viveros
Interior design by Connie Viveros
All photographs by Walusimbi Emmanuel

All proceeds from this book will go to Girl Up Initiative Uganda and their Adolescent Girls Program.

ISBN: 978-1-945363-09-2

Printed in the United States of America

First printing: December 2018

Love-Based Publishing
PO Box 10430
Prescott, Arizona 86304
www.lovebasedpublishing.com

DEDICATION

To the 1.1 billion girls on our planet: We are here for you. We are listening to your stories. Your voices matter.

And to Catherine, age 14, for inspiring the idea of this book project with your desire to be a voice for the voiceless.

TABLE OF CONTENTS

FOREWORD

The Story Behind The Story

How did I, a Western woman, end up in Uganda? Let alone spend six months there? Where did this idea for a book come from? What was it like to collect the stories from the girls? What was it like to take on this book project in Uganda?

Here's a little bit of the story behind the story…

What Called Me To Uganda

When my mom died in July 2016, everything changed. There was no going forward with life "as usual." My grief led me deeper inside, where I began to ask the questions: What is this whole "life" thing really about? What am I uniquely here to contribute?

In response to my inquiry, I sensed the Universe tugging me toward something. (Or perhaps it was the tug that led to my inquiry.) What adventure was I being invited into?

I saw images of myself on the other side of the world, side by side with brown-skinned women and children, involved in their daily activities. I wished to support them, sharing my gifts while learning from them. I wished to plant seeds and grow gardens with them.

I continued my inquiry, listening to the whispers of the Universe and following the breadcrumbs it laid out for me. Over the course of many months, a vision emerged in which I saw myself traveling to East Africa to volunteer with a non-profit engaging in activities that empowered women and girls.

I discovered Girl Up Initiative Uganda (GUIU) online, after exploring many other possible leads and synchronicities After a Skype call with Kimberly Wolf, one of the Co-Founders, we were both "sold" on each other. It was a match. was thrilled!

After our call, I walked away from my computer and gazed out the window in time to see a bright-red cardinal land o the back fence. His vibrant color stood out against the white snowy ground. He sat on the fence for several moment before flying off.

"I'm going to Uganda, Mom," I whispered, as tears streamed down my face. "I'm going to Uganda. Thank you."

Where The Book Idea Came From

I'd had a vision for over a decade of collecting women's stories from all over the world and compiling them into a boo Yet this vision wasn't at the forefront of my conscious mind when I began to volunteer with Girl Up Initiative Ugand

What was at the forefront of my awareness during the first week of volunteering in August 2017 was my desire to d some fundraising for the GUIU Adolescent Girls Program (AGP), so it could be made accessible to more girls.

I asked if I could meet with some of the adolescent girls to hear about their experiences with the program. As I s with Catherine, and then with the twins, Barbra and Bridget, and listened to their stories, that vision of creating compilation of stories that had been lying dormant inside of me for years began to tremble.

On September 2nd, 2017, from a booth at the Café Java in Kampala, I sent an email to Kim (who was in Norway at t time) with the subject line, "I have an idea ..." I shared with her my vision for a book that was comprised of a collecti of the girls' stories that could serve a multitude of functions: a fundraising tool for GUIU, an inspiring example what else is possible in the world, and a wakeup call in regard to the importance of this empowerment work with girls around the world.

From there, the idea snowballed. Kim, Monica (the other Co-Founder), and the AGP coaches (Gloria and Marion) totally supported my idea.

The book began to take on a life of its own.

How We Collected The Girls' Stories

The big question: Would I write the stories, or would the girls write their own? I'm a writer, so I loved the idea of being the one to capture their stories. However, I also loved the idea of empowering the girls to write their own, so we chose that direction and started to plan the first writing workshop.

The first workshop was delivered in the midst of a weekend training for almost 200 girls! There I stood, in front of all these girls, doing my very best to coach them on how to write a few paragraphs about what had changed for them in their lives since joining the Adolescent Girls Program.

Many of the girls didn't speak fluent English. Those who did had a hard time understanding my accent. So Monica and one of the other GUIU coaches, Carol, stood with me, taking turns translating my English into Luganda, the local language.

We were all outside, beneath the hot mid-day sun. Some of the girls were reluctant to write; yet many of them seemed excited by the invitation to share something about themselves. They started scribbling on their pages, so focused, they hardly even looked up. At the end of that short writing workshop, we collected stories from almost half of the girls. I held all their stories close to my chest, deeply touched and looking forward to reading through them all.

Later that night, as I began to read through their pages, I realized I wasn't the "right" one to choose which stories t include in the book. I didn't know the girls the way the AGP team did. So the next day, I invited Monica, Gloria, an Marion to sit and review the stories with me.

It was a rainy afternoon, and we sat together in Monica's office reading through the pages. From time to time, on of the coaches would pause their reading to share something about a story and expand upon it with what she kne about that particular girl. There was laughter, sighs, and even tears that afternoon as we chose the stories we wished t include in the book.

Theirs Is An Oral Tradition

We scheduled a second writing workshop at the GUIU office, and gathered together the girls whose stories had bee chosen to be included in the book. During this time, I awakened to the truth that these girls were not writers; they wer storytellers, growing up in a culture of oral tradition.

So during that second writing workshop, we invited the girls to share more of their stories with us by sitting down an talking one-on-one with one of the GUIU coaches. From there, the coaches typed up their notes, doing their best t capture each girl's story in her own words.

It's a "We" Culture, Not A "Me" Culture

Although the idea originally came through me, this book was truly a collaboration. How could it be any other way? It's a compilation of stories from girls growing up in a "we" culture.

I worked very closely with Gloria, Marion, and Emma (GUIU's Photographer) for months collecting the stories and photos. (The photoshoots could be a whole other book, themselves!)

During this time, I also organized my first online fundraiser, to raise the money required to get our book published and printed. It was such a vulnerable experience to invite my community to contribute money to our project. Yet because it was for such a great cause, I "got over myself," and kept asking.

We ended up raising $6,051 from 84 donors—each dollar of which we're so grateful for, as this money made it possible for you to hold our book in your hands right now!

So this book, every part of it, has been created in collaboration, in the spirit of Ubuntu: "I am because we are."

Ubuntu is an expression from the Zulu Tribe (South Africa). My loose, Western interpretation of this philosophy is, "We're all in this together, so let's do what we can to lift each other up."

Thank you, from the depths of my heart, for taking our book into your hands and reading the stories on these pages. From Monica's and Kim's stories in the introduction, to all of the girls' stories, to mine, my deep desire is that we inspire you to continue to be, do, and contribute what is uniquely yours to the world.

Ubuntu.

The Book Team From Left To Right:
Gloria, Marion, Monica, Kim, Emma & Megan

INTRODUCTION

From Megan Walrod

I sat on a wooden bench in the heat of mid-day in Kampala with sweat on my brow and tears in my eyes as Catherine, age 14, told me, "I want to be the voice of the voiceless. But first I need to learn how to be the voice for myself. That is what Girl Up Initiative Uganda is teaching me to do."

Catherine's wisdom and courage inspired me. In a country where girls are not given a voice or a choice when it comes to issues that directly impact them (such as their bodies, their education, and their futures), this statement was revolutionary. It was also similar to what I had written in my journal in July before leaving to volunteer in Uganda: "I get to be a voice for the voiceless."

As I listened to Catherine tell me more about how Girl Up Initiative Uganda has given her the confidence to say "NO" to sex, avoid the potential risks of early pregnancy and the dangers of childbirth, and focus on her education instead, I started wondering:

What could I do to shine a spotlight on the great work that Girl Up Initiative Uganda is already doing here in Uganda to educate and empower girls?

What could I do to support these girls in finding–and seeing the value of–their voices?

This book is an answer to those questions.

In a world that has silenced girls for too long and still views them as second-class citizens, the stories in this boo
are needed now more than ever. When girls have the opportunity to share their stories, they learn they are valuable
they discover they really do have something to say, and that they can play an essential role in creating cultural shifts
influencing economic development, and eradicating poverty.

When we teach girls the skills required to overcome the daily challenges they face, we support them in unleashing thei
potential, so they can create a better future for all of us. Helping one girl claim her voice advances society as a whole.

Take Monica Nyiraguhabwa, for example, the Co-Founder and Executive Director of Girl Up Initiative Uganda...

From Monica Nyiraguhabwa

I grew up in the slums of Kampala, where poverty is a lived reality.

As a girl, my parents never believed in my education. My dad never thought I would be a great performer. I remembe
one time my father whispered to me, "Monica, you are a beautiful girl, so we don't need to invest so much in you
education. I need to put emphasis on your brother."

When I asked for books, markers, and pens, my dad told me he needed to invest in my brother; that as a girl, one day
man would come and marry me, and take me away to his family. So it was my brother who got the books, pens, fanc
calculator, and geometry set. I wasn't given any supplies. My brother had shoes. I went barefoot. I saw my brother wit
these things and it hurt me. But why? I wondered. Why does he get all of this and I don't?

My self-esteem diminished. I was never the best in class. At one point, I had to repeat class. Not because I was stupi
but because the community, and my own family, wasn't there to encourage me, to support me, and to mentor me.

grew up knowing I was just passing through school.

In my settlement, in the slum, I realized that even my community put limited attention on girls' education. In my primary (elementary) school, I remember a teacher impregnating a girl and of course she didn't have the power to report him. Even if she had reported him, she would be the one they blamed and sent out of school.

When I got to secondary school, I met my high school teacher, Nora, and that was a game-changer. Unlike my parents, she saw something beautiful in me: she identified me as a leader. She told me, "You love people and they love you. You are more of a community person." She saw my gifts and encouraged me to blossom in the areas in which I had natural talents: public speaking, music, and leadership.

Through Nora's mentorship, I found my self-esteem and confidence. I gained the trust and support of the students and was elected into all of the best leadership positions: Student Counselor, Head Girl, and Head of Liturgy. As people began to believe in me and show me love and appreciation, my grades also improved.

When I got accepted into Makerere University (the best university in Uganda) on merit, my name was in the newspaper along with all the other students. My parents looked at my name on that list, saw that I would be getting a degree in Adult and Community Education, and couldn't believe it. How could the daughter who was just passing through school, who had never been given any support or encouragement at home, be excelling?

Can you imagine their shock? The girl from the slums, the girl who couldn't read, the girl who had to repeat class, being given a real chance, because she was coached and mentored by her high school teacher who believed in her.

I excelled in university, and later on received a Commonwealth Scholarship to study at the University College in London. I now have a master's degree in education, gender and international development.

Because of my own experiences and experiences of the girls I've seen grow up in the slums, many of whom droppec out of school because they lacked the mentorship and life skills required to succeed, I decided to start Girl Up Initiative Uganda. Our mentorship programs show me again and again how, when we support and coach a girl, that she car have voice, choice, and ownership over her own body, we're not just changing one girl's life, we're uplifting the entir community.

Monica is an inspiring example of what else is possible when one girl is encouraged to step more fully into he potential. The change she has now catalyzed for thousands of girls is inspiring, and even more importantly, i influencing social norms in Uganda and beyond.

Then there's Kimberly Wolf, Co-Founder and Deputy Executive Director of Girl Up Initiative Uganda, who is a grea example of how potential plus privilege can be a powerful combination for contributing to sustainable change in loca communities…

From Kimberly Wolf

I grew up in a sheltered, privileged, and loving family on the coast of California, in Santa Barbara. I spent summer going between the swimming pool and beach. I played with friends and enjoyed school. I always felt like an explore and wanted to see more of the world to understand it.

I saw poverty for the first time when, at eight years old, we took a family trip to Jamaica. While I had seen homele people in Santa Barbara, they usually moved around with their shopping carts full of belongings. There were als places for them to go to that served warm food and provided shelter. In Jamaica, these shelters weren't as readily available. So many people were living on the streets and seemed to have nothing. I didn't want to leave the hotel because the poverty and sadness in the streets frightened me. How was it possible that people literally had nothing?

One day, my parents got me to leave the hotel room to go on a hike. Our guide was one of the funniest people I'd ever met and was laughing the entire time. How could this man be so happy living amongst so much sadness?

When I was 15 years old, I traveled to Ghana for a summer program. Although I hadn't learnt much at all about Africa in school, the continent called to me. As I walked off the airplane in Accra, the capital city, everyone stared at me. It was my first time experiencing what I imagined it felt like to be a black person in Santa Barbara: all eyes on you because your color is different. I was uncomfortable and intimidated. Yet my summer in Ghana opened my eyes to another way of living, of loving, and of expressing myself that felt so natural to me. While the people I met there were living in poverty, I experienced a sense of gratitude, generosity, happiness, community, and faith that I felt was missing in the lives of people back home. The people of Ghana may have been financially poor, but they were rich in spirit.

When I returned to Santa Barbara, I knew I was not the same person I was when I'd left, and that I'd never be the same again. I didn't want to integrate back into a society that felt a bit sad to me, that felt like it needed a bit of African energy and life in it. My time in Ghana ignited an urge in me to learn more about why Africa was such an amazing-yet-misunderstood continent. Why did all the images of Africa portray sadness, hunger, and poverty, when there was so much beauty, color, and love?

My travels inspired my educational path. I studied International Development at UC Berkeley. I spent a year studying abroad in South Africa, during which time I also traveled in Western and Southern Africa. The more I learnt about Africa, the more I learnt about myself, and the more I became aware of how I could use my privilege to amplify the voices of African people and create a bridge between the two worlds that I inhabited.

I also noticed that women bore the brunt of poverty while taking care of five or six children. It became clear that without access to accurate sexual and reproductive information and contraceptives, girls would follow the same cycl of poverty, and never have opportunities for a different future.

I began having a vision of partnering with a young woman in an African country to start an organization for youn women, run by young women, focusing on sexual reproductive health, rights, and gender awareness. I knew that, fo an organization such as this to be effective and sustainable, the programming would need to come from women in th community.

So when I went to Uganda to volunteer in my early 20's, it was as though fate brought Monica and I together.

We met at another women's rights organization where we were both working. When I returned from visiting a slur one day, Monica approached me to see how it had been for me. I told her I was appalled. I was especially shocked b how dangerous it was for girls. I saw girls wearing torn-up clothing, wandering around looking for food rather tha attending school. Older girls were dressed up and earning money as sex workers.

Monica took me to visit the slum where she grew up. We visited with young mothers between the ages of 16-18 year They didn't know what to do with their children, or where to get money for their next meal. Their desperation wa palpable. I realized how much they needed hope and opportunities for a better future for themselves and their childre

These visits fueled the fire that had been burning inside of me all along. I was determined to find ways to support th young women who had so much potential, but who didn't have the encouragement, support, and economic means reach their dreams.

As we left that day, an idea ignited between us. What if Monica and I joined forces to advocate for adolescent girls and young women growing up in the slums? What might we create if we combined my privilege with her local acumen?

I was leaving the next week for South Africa to begin working toward my master's degree, so there wasn't time to develop our idea further, together. However, Monica promised me that if I left her with a bit of money, she would start the work. So I left her with $100 USD as an investment in our shared vision.

Monica and I stayed in touch daily. Within a few weeks, Monica had already started offering business training and support to young mothers. Within a few months, she began mentorship and life skills training in our first school, and enrolled 50 girls in the program. Our idea had become a reality!

What started off as a conversation and an investment of $100 USD has now turned into a registered non-profit organization, a team of 15+ staff and volunteers. At the time of the writing in 2018, we've reached 1,475 girls, 193 young women, and 94,623 youth through our programs. We're growing and expanding every single day and seeing the "ripple effects" of our efforts.

Monica and I came up with the name "Girl Up" on the taxi ride home after our visit to the slum that afternoon. We wanted the name of our organization—whatever it ended up being—to reflect our commitment to lifting girls up out of a life of poverty and gender inequality as we invited them to own (and be proud of) their authenticity and strength. Just as boys are taught to "man up," we wanted girls to be taught to "girl up," and realize their power as females!

In the collective culture of Uganda, people around you have a big influence on how you understand yourself, as wel as your life choices. We see again and again how, when these adolescent girls are given resources, knowledge, an mentorship, they become advocates for themselves and those around them. They stand up for their rights and speak u about the issues that impact them while sharing their knowledge with other girls. In the process, they are challengin gender norms and power dynamics and becoming change agents in their communities.

Together, we are contributing to creating a brighter future for each Girl Up girl. Since you are reading this book, yo too are joining us in this transformational change. As one of our GUIU Coaches said, "Young adolescent girls love t be heard and listened to. It gives them a sense of belonging to our world and society."

By investing in our book, by reading each of the girls' stories inside, you are contributing to the global solution empowering adolescent girls and letting them know their voices matter. They have something to say, and you ar letting them know that you are listening.

GIRLS' STORIES

"I now know how to say 'No' without my eyes saying 'Yes'."

Akiror Flavia Bernadeth
Age 12

There lived a girl. When she was in the village for her holiday, boys used to ask her for sex, but she would say, "I am still young. Please, leave me alone."

But she became friendly to them and closer to them. One day, she was walking towards a nearby bush to look for firewood. Those boys were following her when she did not know.

They caught up with her and said, "Today you are alone; let's see whether you will run away." They said, "Do you want to keep this, or you want to do it, so you can be free?"

She said, "NO," but her eyes were saying, "YES" so the boys caught her and said, "You are lying. Your eyes are saying 'yes.'"

They tried to have sex with her, but they never know how to do it. She was saved because they never knew what to do.

That girl used to like to move with bad peer groups. Now she is in Girl Up.

That girl was me.

Now I know how to say "No" without my eyes saying "Yes."

When I grow up, I want to become a doctor, because I always see people dying and I feel bad when I see people dying because of poor medical services. I want to help people to live a better, healthy life. I really feel sorry for pregnant mothers who die in pain because of lack of midwives to help them give birth, and sometimes, their bodies die because of poor hygiene. I want to become a doctor to advise young girls who become pregnant because of love for boys. I want to help pregnant mothers give birth to a healthy, lovely baby.

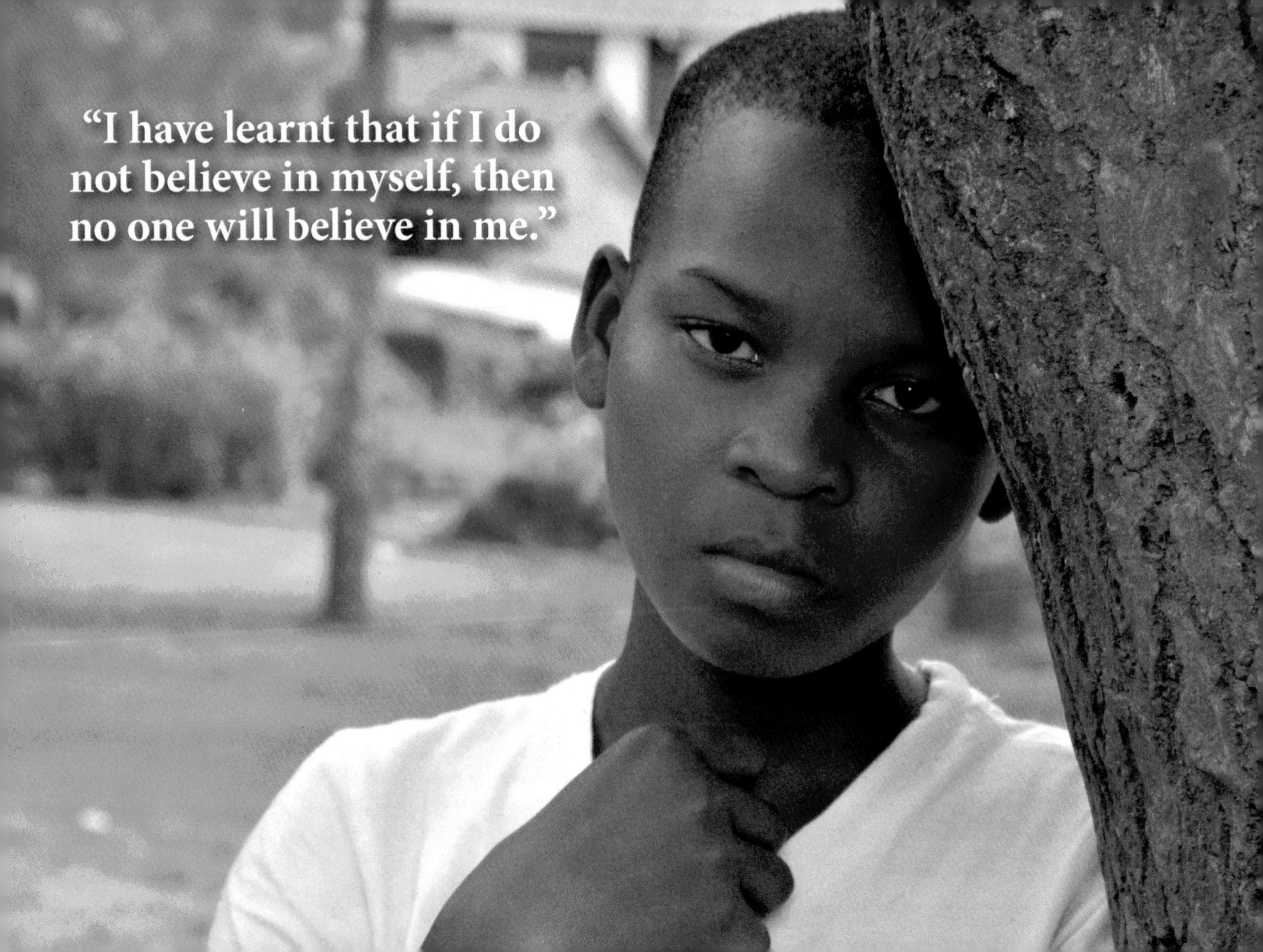
"I have learnt that if I do
not believe in myself, then
no one will believe in me."

Nalunga Aisha
Age 13

When I was in Primary 4, I had just joined Kiswa Primary School and did not know anyone there. There was a group of three girls who had been in the school already, and they did not like me. They made fun of me because of my stutter, and they said that I was not bright enough. I remained without a friend and thought that everyone thought of me the same way. At home, we are eight children, so I decided to remain friends with just my siblings at home.

I had low self-esteem and feared speaking out. I was shy and felt left out because my classmates used to abuse me, and I felt lonely. There were some pupils who used to do bad things, and I thought that I am also bad like them, because of my low self-esteem. I was not confident to speak out by myself because I thought people will abuse me like my classmates used to do.

When I was like that, I thought, "I am not a good child," so I decided to join the bad peer groups. They influenced me by making me do bad things. I started abusing people. This was because I did not know myself.

When I was in Primary 5, the people from Girl Up Initiative Uganda came and introduced their club to us. I did not believe in what they were saying. I thought they were joking and could not take it seriously. I also did not want to be anywhere else where people would make fun of me.

But one day, my female teachers asked me, "Why don't you join Girl Up?" I could not refuse because I liked it, but I was shy and feared to speak out. When those of Girl Up came, I feared because I could not get used to being with such caring people. They were kind to everyone.

They taught us so many good things and very many topics. Out of those topics, I most liked self-esteem, because th
topic helped me to know myself and to be confident, so that I can speak out by myself without fearing anything.
could not believe that I can speak for myself. It was unbelievable, but I believed it. I know I can teach others to belie
in themselves.

One time at home, my mom asked me what had changed about me, because she realised that I was happier and not
loner anymore. I told her that it is because of Girl Up Initiative Uganda, and that I have learnt that if I do not belie
in myself, then no one will believe in me.

The same girls who used to tease me are now my friends, because they also later on joined Girl Up and we were taug
how to live with others and respect everyone. They no longer make fun of me and we get along well, and they
not mind my stuttering anymore. I am no longer a sad girl. I am a member of the school health club now, and I c
confidently talk to them when we are doing our activities.

I want to become a doctor so that I can help those people who cannot treat themselves. I want to help my parents
have a good and healthy life. I want to help the orphans who lost their parents. I also want to help those people w
stay on the streets. I want to help young girls who don't know what they are to realise their dreams, and to promote g
child education so that they can have a better future.

"I became my mother's coach."

Akumu Faith
Age 12

When my family moved from the village to the city, I joined Girl Up. However, my elder cousin (age 17) discouraged me from being part of the club. She and another boy in the neighbourhood made fun of me for being part of the club. One time my mom heard her bullying me about being part of Girl Up, and stopped her. My mother encouraged me to continue being in Girl Up so that when I get back home, I share what we have learnt during the session. She told my cousins that if I failed to share with them what I had learnt, I would then be stopped from attending the trainings and being in the club.

My favourite sessions were life skills and peer pressure, and the mentorship training for the Big Sisters. My cousin would say that I am big-headed and make fun of my body features like my feet, or for not being cool and nice. The life skills helped me to go through this kind of treatment because the coaches taught us how to appreciate our bodies for what they do for us and that each body part plays an important role to the functioning of the whole body. I told my cousin that if only she had read my book of notes from Girl Up, she would not have the mentality she had and would also change how she talks to me. She told me mockingly to give her the book and when she was done reading through my notes, she stopped calling me names and even apologised for how she had previously treated me.

Before Girl Up, I was a loner and did not like to associate with people or even talk to them. But through Girl Up, I learnt that we need to live with others and that living with people is important.

My mother was going through a lot of stress and social pressure. She was not happy. Whenever I shared the skills we had learnt from the trainings, she was interested in knowing the details, so I became her coach. I did not miss explaining any of the sessions because my mother was also always looking forward to learning what I learnt.

My mother was also not confident while talking to people. She would look down to answer, but now, she faces peop in the eyes. My mother also liked the session about peer pressure and when I taught her about it, she learnt how overcome the social pressures from her relatives who were constantly influencing her decisions. My mother is no able to say “NO” confidently to her relatives who try to get her to do things she does not want to do, or who scare h about what bad they can do to her.

I want everyone to know my story and let them learn from me as I learn from them. Let us all learn from each oth and learn how to help others. I also want others to be proud of themselves and start speaking up for themselves.

My dream is to become a lawyer because I want to save my mum’s land from land grabbers.

"I want to help other girls."

Amooti Florence
Age 12

My name is Amooti Florence. I come from a family of five, but two sisters of mine are married which makes us three left at home. My father does not stay at home with us. He told me he is going to Jinja to work. My father comes home once a month. Life at home is not good, because my mother struggles to pay for school fees and food.

I was unable to speak out before joining the Adolescent Girls Program. This happened to me especially with my mother and my classmates. I feared speaking out to my mother because she was very tough. She used to beat me. She didn't want me to go to church. She wouldn't give me money for food. I stayed at school and didn't eat. When I went back home, she told me to go back to Jinja where my dad was. "I don't need you here. You go and tell somebody to give you a home where you can stay."

My mother was not tough before, but became tough when my big sister got pregnant. My sister was in Senior 2 when she got pregnant. This changed my mother's attitude and I started fearing her. This affected me to a point that I feared my teachers and my classmates and I would never participate in class.

When I joined the Adolescent Girls Program, the coaches taught me how to speak out. During the sessions, the coaches would always bring us before the others and encourage us to talk. That was how I started being assertive. The first day I realised I could speak out was when I had a one-on-one conversation with my mother. She was very happy to know that I am no longer as shy as before. I also teach my neighbors and my friends in Sunday School. They were also unable to speak out before, but I am glad that they are able to speak out after I taught them what the coaches taught me.

My mother also forgave my sister after she attended the Parents' Meeting at Girl Up Initiative Uganda. The coache encouraged the parents to give their children a safe space for sharing and to also forgive them when they do wron actions. She also told me she would not continue to beat me.

When I grow up, I want to be a coach of Girl Up. I want to help other girls because some girls are too young to g pregnant. Some of them get pregnant in school. When they produce, they could have their mother beat them, askin "Why do you produce when you are still young?" And the child, it might be a mistake, but the mother or stepmoth could take the baby and not give you food, school fees, and books. She might not buy a uniform for you. Most of th girls get pregnant because they lack people to guide them and talk to them. I want to be that person who talks to then

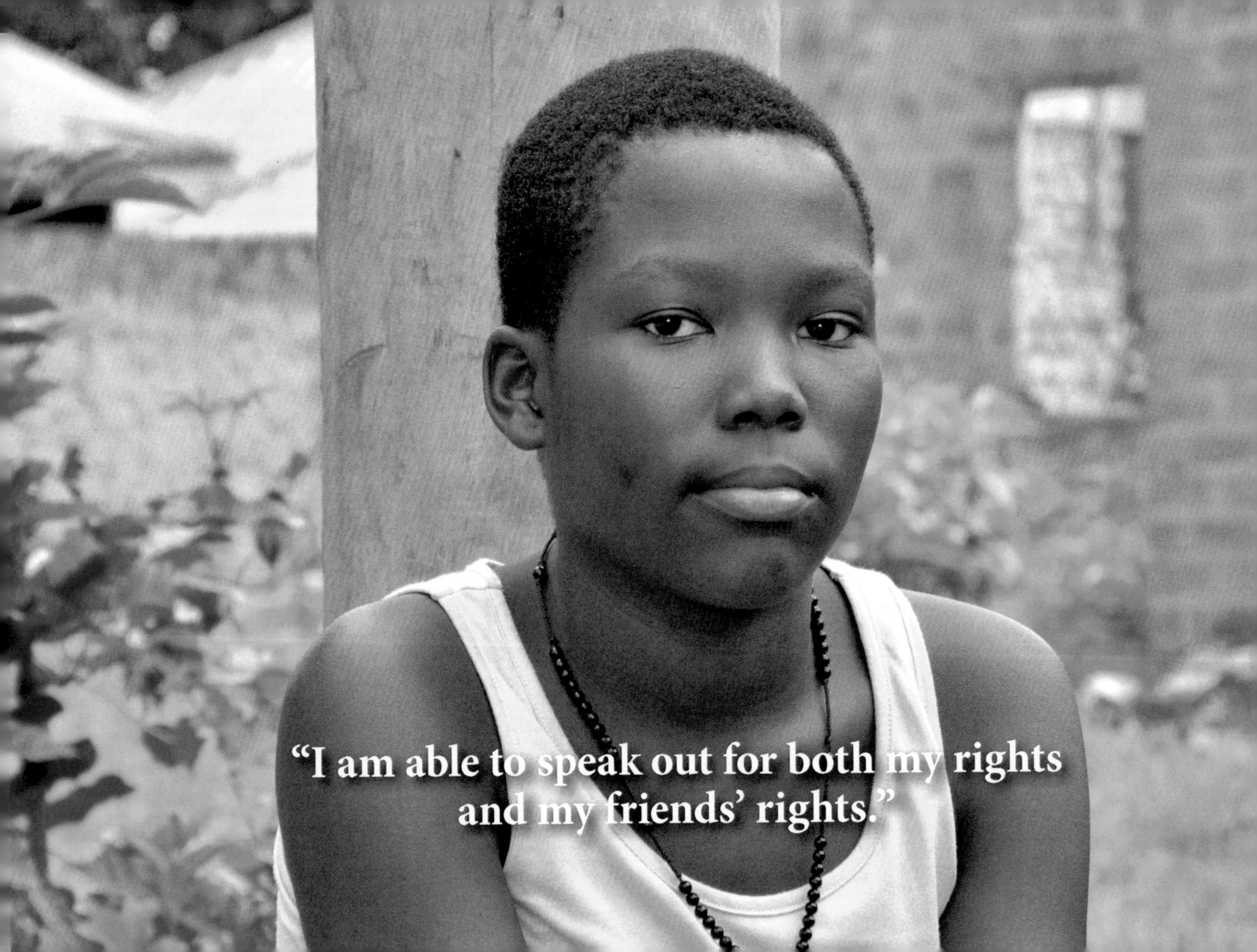
"I am able to speak out for both my rights
and my friends' rights."

Naigaga Joan
Age 13

My name is Naigaga Joan. I am thirteen years old. I come from a family of four. That is to say two girls and two boys of which I am the first born.

When we moved from the village to the city, we had a small house and were still renting. I found there two friends. But as I got to know them, they became bad to me. They started teasing me that I was a village girl and didn't know anything.

I started abusing them, doing everything which is bad. I also became tough and had no control of my temper. I would always get into fights with my friends and siblings. Whenever I got into fights with my siblings, my mother would beat me, and this made me more furious.

When I joined the Adolescent Girls Program, the first session we had was about being assertive. The coaches taught us how to be assertive rather than being aggressive. Aggressive is when someone talks harshly and abuses others. Assertive is when you can express yourself and are confident enough to stand up and talk.

It is through this that I realised that my temper was an aggressive behavior and I needed to work on it. I learnt how to cool my temper by doing something that makes me happy, like sing or dance. The coaches helped me change. I am now an assertive and confident girl. I am able to speak out for both my rights and my friends' rights.

Like one time when my younger brothers told me, "You see this girl, Joan, she's just big for nothing." My moth
thought I was going to beat them, so she started beating me. I stood up to her and said, "Mom, I haven't done anythin
You just leave me. I haven't beaten them." And she stopped beating me.

I have a friend whose grandmother keeps beating her for nothing. They give her hard work to do and her uncles a
just sitting there doing nothing. I went to her grandmother and told her to stop violating the girl. The grandmoth
yelled at me saying I know nothing; that the girl's father died, and she is now responsible for her. I told my mom to
and talk with the grandmother and she did. Now, the grandmother doesn't beat my friend anymore.

Through Girl Up Initiative Uganda, I was renewed, like the morning rays to the surface. They gave me hope to rise a
shine again.

I am sharing my story because I want to help girls get their rights back. They are abused and violated. I want to spe
out for them for they are voiceless. I want to share my story with other people, so they can know more about very ma
things and their self-esteem. I want them to stop being aggressive and be assertive.

I dream of being a doctor. I want to reduce the rate of infant mortality. I want to break the myth that only females a
good in kitchens. I want them to know that all women can do everything. I want to reduce the rate of diseases li
cancer in Uganda. I want to treat people who can't afford medical care for themselves.

"I have learnt to
be confident and
to speak out on
anything that is not
comfortable for me."

Nakandi Shaluwa
Age 13

When I was in Primary 5, I was a bright girl. I was the first in class and I was very confident to speak out in class.

But one day, when I was going back home, I met a group of boys. One of the boys told me that he loves me. The others told me they would not let me through and that they would beat me up for not accepting to be in a relationship with one of them. I did not know what to do because I was alone, so I decided to tell them that I agree to be in a relationship with one of the boys. However, deep in my heart, I knew that I did not want this, and I did not mean what I had said. I only wanted to get past them so that I could get home.

When I got home, I did not tell my mother about it because I was scared. The next day, I never wanted to go back to school. My mother told me, "Shaluwa, wake up and go to school." In my heart I said, "Won't I meet the boys on my way when I'm going back to school?" But it was a must to go to school for the end-of-year exams.

During the holidays, the boys would come and hang around our house. Every time I noticed them there, I tried to hide so they wouldn't see me. But if they did see me, they'd call to me to come out and I'd go meet them.

When we got our reports from school, my mother was very annoyed because I used to perform well, but because I joined the bad peer groups, I performed very poor.

In Primary 6, I joined Girl Up Initiative Uganda. They told us about bad peer groups, low self-esteem, and to avoid early marriage. They taught us about speaking out against violence, and that if we do not speak out against violence, then the effect could be worse than if we had talked earlier.

I thought about the boys that told me they love me. I hate the boys. So I told my mother about what had bee
happening with the boys and she was shocked. She told me that she would start giving me money for transportatio
from school to take me home so the boys would not follow me home. She also told me that in case these boys appeare
again around our home, I should tell her so that she faces them and asks them what they want.

She started giving me transport money and the boys did not have a chance to follow me again on my way home. An
when they showed up near our home, they found my mother, and she confronted them and told them that she woul
report them to the police if they came back again. Although the boys tried to deny the accusations, my mother tol
them to back off. From then on, the boys did not disturb me again, and they even fear me at school when they see m

I was promoted to Primary 7. I love my studies and Girl Up Initiative Uganda because they helped me to have sel
esteem, be confident, and avoid bad peer groups. I have learnt to be confident and to speak out on anything that is n
comfortable for me. I love my coaches and parents.

When I finish studying, I want to be a doctor, treat sick people, and save people's lives.

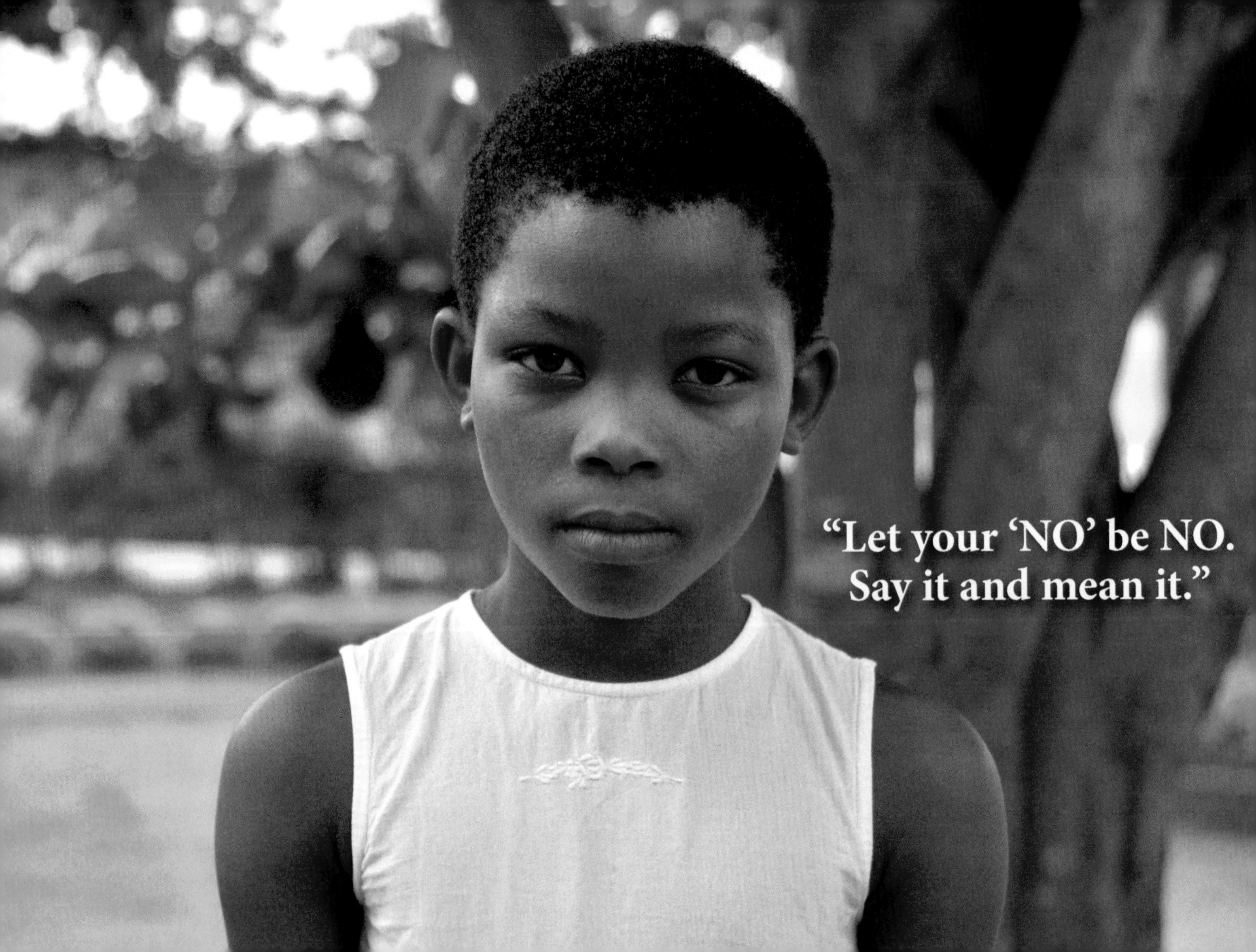
“Let your ‘NO’ be NO.
Say it and mean it.”

Namukasa Tracy
Age 11

I used to be fearful of people, including visitors and my parents as well. Being the last born, I would get away with it, because people considered me to be a naturally-shy girl. When visitors came over, I would stay in the house and not go out to greet them.

I was also very playful, and I would play till late even though it is not good for young children to be playing out in the night. My grandmother would tell me that it wasn't good for children to be playing that late in the night, but I wouldn't listen. I was a short girl but very stubborn.

I was also very short-tempered and easily started up fights in our neighbourhood. I didn't control myself. I was someone who wanted to fight every moment. When someone told me something bad that I didn't want to hear, I just beat him or her. But when he was bigger than me, I'd throw a stone at him and run away. I had learnt all these kinds of behaviours from my friends back in the village.

But when I joined Girl Up Initiative Uganda, they taught us how to practise speaking amidst big numbers of people because the club had over 80 girls. I stopped being fearful of people and even at home, I began being the first person to go out and greet people who have just come home. My grandmother was amused.

I learnt how to make friends and not let them decide what I should or should not be doing. I learnt about all the things that may happen to me as a girl if I continue to play out in the night, so I do not play late in the night anymore.

I have also learnt how to control my anger so that I do not end up in fights. When someone tells me something bad, just say, "Stop those bad things you are doing." If they don't stop, I just leave him or her, or I report him to a big person I feel good not abusing people anymore.

I have used the skills I learnt from Girl Up Initiative Uganda to help my young nephew. He used to just take ou grandmother's money without asking for it and then deny that he had been the one who had taken the money. I kne that it was not a good thing to do, so I mentored him and told him that it is not good, until he stopped it.

I want to share my story with other people to learn from me. People, they are shy, and I was, but now I'm not shy. want them to learn from me not to be shy.

I also want girls to know that if a boy comes and says, "I love you," the girl might say, "I don't love you," and she's sh The boys know that her "NO" may mean "YES," and the boy will come and disturb you every day. You need to sa "NO," assertively. Let your "NO" be NO. Say it and mean it. Even when you're saying that "NO," make eye contact. Sa "NO."

When I grow up, I want to be a doctor to treat sick people and help those who cannot help themselves. I want to he people. Girl Up Initiative Uganda is helping me do this.

“I began to do things that
I did not believe I could.”

Namulemeri Cissy
Age 12

Once upon a time, I, a girl who has seven sisters and three brothers (some are step-siblings), lived a terrible life because my parents were poor and couldn't provide me with whatever I needed. As a girl, I needed things, like pads and clothes.

My parents are always having quarrels because of the children. They are always disagreeing on who is treating the other's children badly. My father thinks that my mom sometimes discriminates the children that she has not given birth to and then he starts a quarrel and my mom also does the same which ends up causing all the arguments. This has been a challenge for us, because we sometimes fail to ask for what we want because our parents are always having fights over who has what and who doesn't.

As a girl, I faced many problems at school, especially when I was in Primary 5, because that is when my menstruation periods began. Without any knowledge, blood would go onto my skirt and the boys teased me, nicknaming me names like "Miss Blood."

I could not talk to my parents about it or even ask for help from them. It was shaming for me and it always made me feel uncomfortable. I would get my uniform stained and children at school would laugh at me. Sometimes, I didn't even go to school and I know there are many girls facing the same problem. To tell you the truth, I felt like I should drop out of school.

One day when the same thing happened again, a friend of mine who was much older took me to the senior woman teacher, who helped to explain what was happening to me and she gave me sanitary towels to use. Then, fortunately, the Girl Up Initiative Uganda Program came to teach us about the facts about girls which we didn't know, like how

every normal woman experiences menstruation periods. After joining Girl Up, I learnt that teasing and the nickname
should not make me give up on my education.

Sometimes, when my mother is not in the worst moods, I can ask her for sanitary pads. I also learnt how to mak
reusable sanitary pads from Girl Up Initiative Uganda.

I was a former headgirl of my school and on learning how to make reusable sanitary pads, I unlearnt a belief tha
I would never help any girl. But after Girl Up Initiative Uganda, I talked to our senior woman teacher who had th
idea of teaching other girls who had not been part of the Girl Up training on how to make reusable sanitary pads. W
started teaching girls how to make these, but before that, I would carry my extra pair of uniforms to school so that, i
case a girl got hers stained by her period, I would share my extra pair with her to keep her from being ashamed.

I learnt to understand my body from Girl Up, to believe in myself, and communicate to people. I have learnt t
maintain eye contact and also avoid peer pressure. I also began to do things that I did not believe I could. At school,
have not only been helping girls who have challenges, but also the boys who need help. I even teach boys how to mak
pads.

Sometimes as a leader in school, children would talk to me about a challenge they have at home, and perhaps the onl
way to help them is to approach the teachers and ask them to talk to the child's parents, which the child wouldn't hav
done for themselves.

Now, I have just completed my Primary 7 and I am happy. I want to go to Kyambogo College for Secondary School.
know there are many girls who are facing the same problems I did, so I tell them "Girls don't lose hope, and never giv
up from your studies." I did not give up and now I am a girl who is studying.

I want to become a lawyer, because I want to help the women who are imprisoned, mistreated, and tortured. I also want to help those who are imprisoned for nothing and fight corruption in my country, so that even the poor can get justice. I want to fight for human rights, especially for the women, because I see they are the ones who are most violated. And lastly, I want to become the first woman chief justice of Uganda.

"Standing up for yourself is best."

Namboowa Viola
Age 12

In Primary 6, I was very short, and boys used to tease me, calling me "Luswatha" (meaning "You are too short and won't become tall"). It hurt me a lot. There was a boy called Don who was the leader. When I'd go back home after school, I'd cry because I didn't have the confidence to speak out and say to Don to leave me alone in peace.

My performance was good because I used to be the second and sometimes the first in class. I made sure that he wouldn't beat me, although he was among the first five people.

Don made my life miserable. I even didn't want to go to school some days. I hated my body, because all the other people were tall, but only I was short.

I felt uncomfortable with my body, nd wondered why I was short and the only short girl in our class. What surprised me was that Don was also short, so I wondered how a short boy could call me short. He would get away with it because his father was a teacher in the school, and therefore, reporting would not make any big difference.

One day my mother had no more money to pay for my school fees. So she decided to take me to a new school. She thought that I would cry, but instead I said, "Thank you." I didn't tell her the reason why, but only me and my former classmates knew the reason.

When I came to my new school in Primary 7, Girl Up Initiative Uganda taught us how to be confident and how t
appreciate our bodies. I learnt you should appreciate your body even if you're short. There are people who don't hav
the body you have. If you're admiring other people's bodies, you need to know you have the best body. Other peopl
might not have legs to walk on, so I appreciate my short legs. Now I can enjoy everything. Even if you tease me, I sa
"That is how I was created."

When we went to a netball competition, Don was also there and tried to tease me again. This time, I told him wit
confidence to leave me alone and that I appreciate my body. In the next competition, he never teased me again. I fe
good because standing up for yourself is best. I felt a lift from a burden.

I want other girls to hear my story so that they can have more confidence and know that they're not the only one
passing through that difficult situation. Even us. We find a way of overcoming them. They should also find a way o
overcoming them by being confident and saying "NO" assertively. Boys should also respect girls. Even girls are huma
beings and should not be viewed as animals.

When I grow up, I want to be a heart surgeon. I see so many people with heart problems flying to India to be treate
as if we cannot do it ourselves. I want to be able to treat them from here and also want others to come here to g
treatment. I want Uganda to be known to have the best doctor for heart problems.

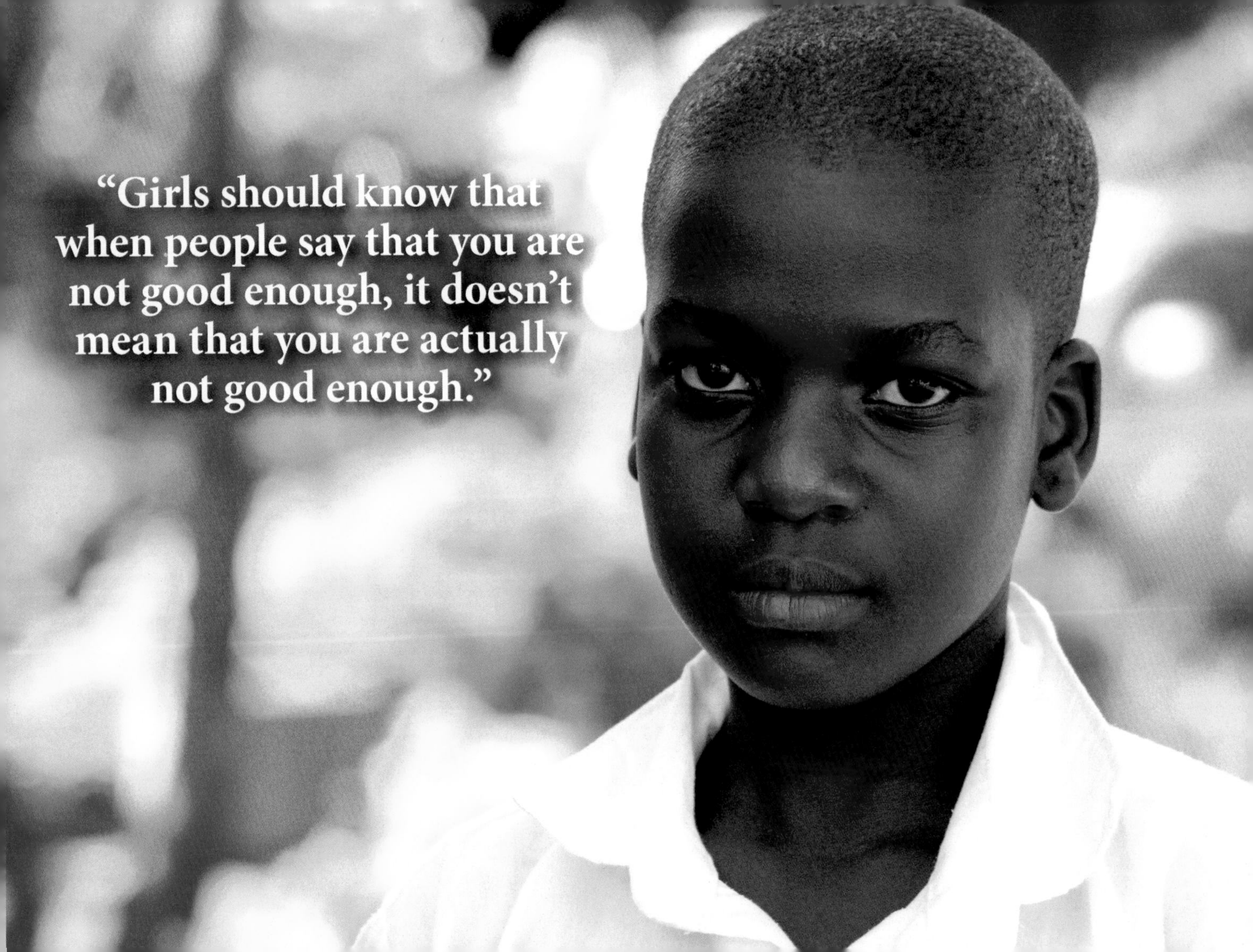
"Girls should know that
when people say that you are
not good enough, it doesn't
mean that you are actually
not good enough."

Awori Victoria
Age 10

I used to stay with my stepmother because my mother had separated from my father. Because my mom had two children at that time, she decided to leave for the village with my elder sister, so that she could help her out with housework and any other things. She left me with my dad's new wife. My mother promised me before she left that she was going to work hard and make sure that she gets a house, so that she can come back for me and we can stay together.

My stepmother mistreated me and called me names. I cooked the food that my dad bought, but she would never give me any of it to eat. One day, she locked me out of the house, and I almost spent the whole night out on the veranda. Luckily, that night, my mother had travelled to come to Kampala to see how I was doing. When she found me seated out in the middle of the night, she asked me what happened, and I told her the story. She knocked at the door, but my stepmother did not open up. My mom then took me to one of her sisters who was also living in Kampala, and that was where we spent the night. She asked her sister if I could stay with them for some time while she continues to look for a job, to which my aunt agreed.

I had only spent a few days with them, my mother had already travelled back to the village, and because my stepmother got to know about where I was staying, she came to my auntie's place and forcefully took me away. She claimed that it was on my father's order, which left my aunt with no option but to give me back to her. On return to her home, she mistreated me even worse. She tried to stop me from going to school, but I would escape from home to go and attend class. When my mom sent money from the village to pay for my school fees, my stepmother instead paid for her children, knowing that if I defaulted paying the school fees, I would be chased from school and wouldn't be going anywhere.

During that time, I had just joined the Girl Up Club, so I found myself coming late for the trainings, but I learnt hov to be strong and live through the difficult situation. I learnt to believe in myself and not believe the bad words an negative declarations that my stepmother would make about me. I also learnt how to be responsible, because of th many times that my mother had been sending school fees money and my stepmother was misusing it. So one time m aunt advised my mom to send the money to her, and she handed me the money to pay directly to the school withou letting my stepmother know about how and where the money had come from.

My mother later on got a job and relocated to Kampala. She came to my stepmother's home and got me to go and sta with her. I was very happy, because I knew that I was not going to go through what my stepmother had been takin me through. I was excited, because even by the time my mother took me back, I had learnt through Girl Up Initiativ Uganda to be confident, to study hard, and believe more in myself. I was a very bright girl in class, always taking firs position, but because my stepmother always said that I was stupid and had only cheated to get the good grades, I a some point felt like studying hard and being bright was pointless. But I'm greatful that Girl Up Initiative Uganda cam in at the right time to encourage me, which helped me to live through my hard time that I was having even whe people did not know about everything that was happening.

I want to share my story because I know that many girls who do not live with their parents suffer a lot and are denie so many opportunities, yet they have the ability to do well and be better girls. Other girls, they are not proud themselves. I want to raise my voice for other voices. Girls should know that when people say that you are not goo enough, it doesn't mean that you are actually not good enough.

I dream of becoming a doctor in the future, so I can treat people in my country and put an end to the dangerou diseases that kill people.

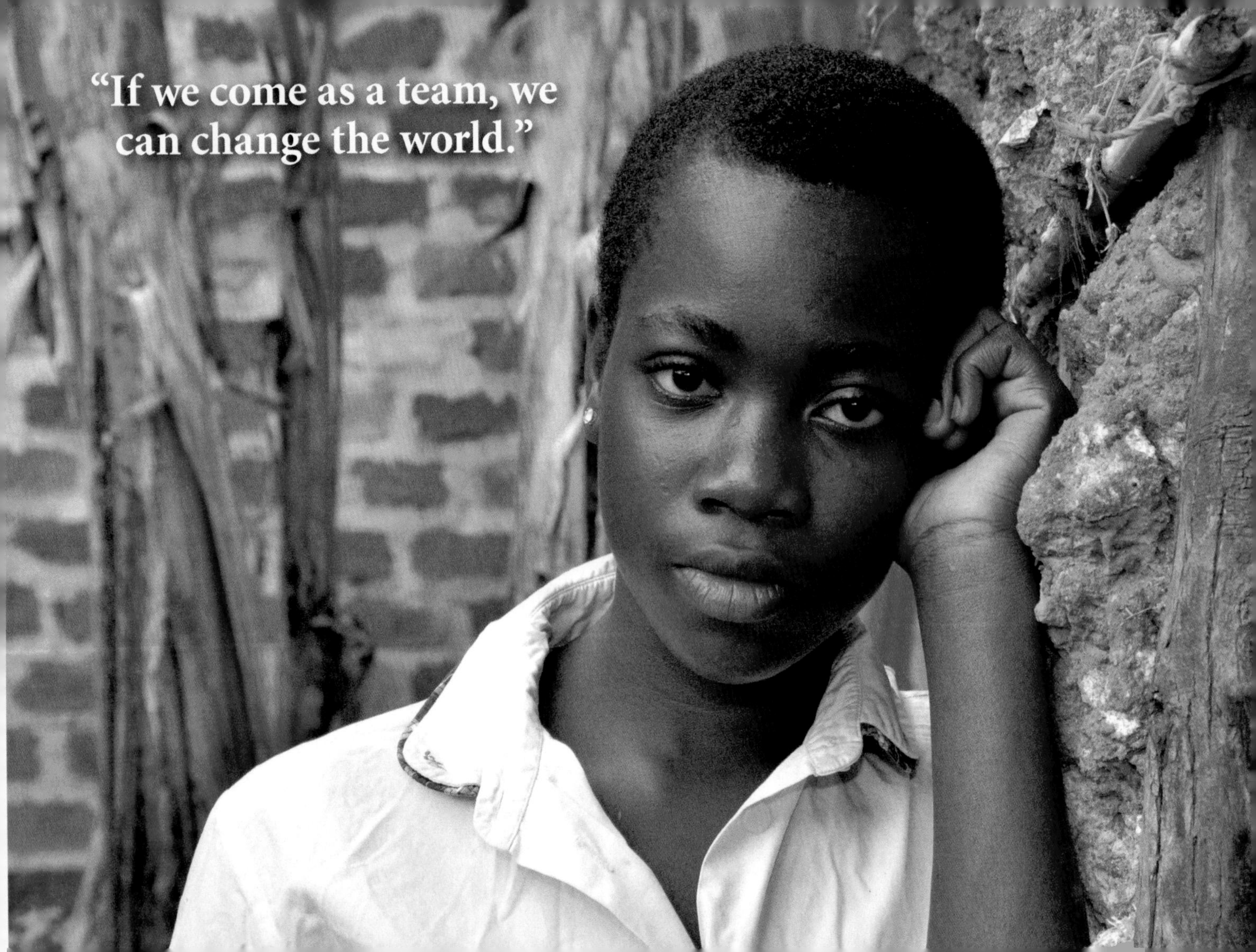
"If we come as a team, we can change the world."

Aromorach Maria
Age 15

I come from a slum called "Manyatta." Life in Manyatta is not easy because when it rains, our house, which is made of mud, gets flooded, and the iron sheets leak. We put basins where it leaks and get more basins from the neighbors and then the house can't get wet much.

I live with my mom and stepdad. I have a younger sister and three brothers. If we're doing work, we do all of it at once as a team. My mom tells us if we work as a team, you make a proper thing at home. We do everything together. Our house is clean. Our compound is clean.

Before joining the Adolescent Girls Program I didn't know why my mom gave me drugs every morning. I finally asked her, "Why am I the only one taking drugs? My brothers aren't taking any medicine." But she wouldn't tell me why.

When I joined the Adolescent Girls Program, we were taught how to be confident and how to speak out. They said if your mom is hiding something from you, go to her and ask, "Mom, what is this?" Know the truth.

After some time, I decided to approach my mother. So one day when I came back from Girl Up, I said, "Mom, why do you give me, every day, pills?"

She said, "Where did you get these questions from? You've become over-confident, asking me these questions. Why do you want to know?"

I told her the coaches encouraged us to always speak out. I said, “I want to know. I am already a grown-up girl by being confident.”

She told me, “You’re HIV positive. Your life is dependent on your medicine.”

The moment I got to know about my status, I hated myself. But with the continued support and encouragement from the Girl Up Initiative Uganda coaches, I gained back my confidence and as I speak, I am proud of myself. I take my medicine properly. I don’t want to give up.

I want my friends to achieve their dreams the way Girl Up Initiative Uganda helps me to achieve my dreams. Like, never knew I could sing. I was in the church. I used to just pray and go back home. But one day, Coach Monica cam and said, “If you know how to sing and dance, you can come.” “Me?” I asked. “I don’t know how to do anything.” Sh said, “You have to be confident as a girl. No fearing. You have to be assertive.”

I tried. They told me I have talent. I can dance. At church they said, “You can sing. You have a talent. Join the choir Now I sing and I’m a soloist.

I am excited to share my story to let boys and girls not think they’re the only ones with that problem they’re passin through. They should never give up. There is no problem you can’t solve. Every problem has a solution.

People should know you have to work for it. Work, and then you’ll get it. Me, if I want my problem to go away, I can just sit and want it to go away. No. You have to do something.

We can change. But one voice cannot change. Meaning, me alone, I cannot change the world. But if we come as a team we can change the world.

Girl Up
Initiative
“Be proud of yourself as a girl

Amanicia Spencer
Age 12

When I joined school, I did not have friends from Primary 1 to Primary 6. I did not know how to make friends. I would just go to school and back home. Even the other children in school did not approach me to be their friend, because I was just an ordinary girl. I did not know how to impress people.

In our class, there was a group of boys who used to bully and tease me because of my language. They all considered Lugbara (a language spoken in the West Nile region in northwestern Uganda) to be the worst language in the world. Whenever they would hear Lugbara, they would laugh and abuse the language. They said it sounded horrible and that people from my tribe must be stupid. That really made me feel I am so unlucky to be a Lugbara. Since I was the only Lugbara in almost the whole class, I felt really bad about what they were saying.

I am dark-skinned, and boys used to abuse me because of my colour, and even girls would do the same, so that really discouraged me from trying to make friends. I thought no light-skinned person can ever be my friend, because of my dark skin.

I did have one friend that year, but in Primary 7, we were separated because we were in different classrooms. She got new friends. Because I did not bring money for snacks and her new friends used to bring for her what to eat at breaktime, she just started avoiding me. That hurt me so much, because she was my only friend. But for her, she didn't care, because she already had friends.

One bright morning, when I was feeling so lonely, one of the coaches from Girl Up came to our school and told us about their club. I was so happy to become a member of Girl Up, although my challenge was not yet solved. But time went on and one day, the coaches taught us about having self-esteem, having confidence, and appreciating our bodies and best of all, I learnt how to make friends.

My confidence improved, and I started talking to people and approaching them myself. I was able to talk to m classmates without fear and look in their eyes when talking to them. I started giving them good advice and that helpe me make many friends.

I was also able to stand up to those who were making fun of me. I told them, "Just because I'm a Lugbara does not mea I'm not a human being. We have the same blood. I'm proud of what I am." They left me alone after I stood up to them

I started joining teams, like netball. I love netball. My teacher picked me to be the Class Monitor, and had me shar messages with the whole class.

Right now, as I speak, I have unlimited confidence, I love my body and my tribe for who I am, and I have very man friends. All thanks to Girl Up.

If my sister came to me and said, "It's hard being a girl," I would tell her we're really lucky to be girls. Our bodies a unique from the boys. And that life goes good when you learn how to take care of yourself and be proud of yourse as a girl.

I am excited to share my story because I wish all other girls out there will learn from my story that they are not differe from other girls at all. I love you all.

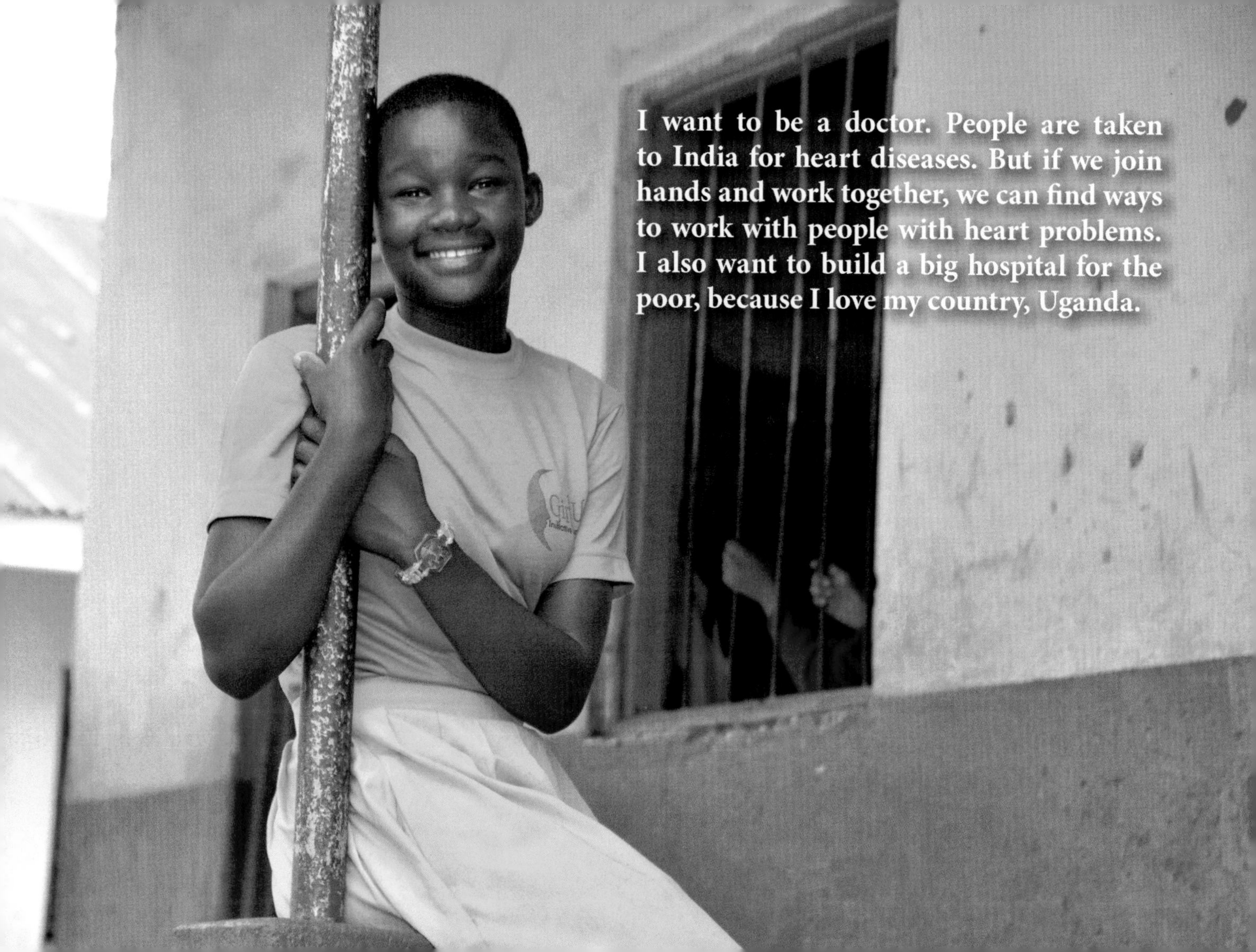

I want to be a doctor. People are taken to India for heart diseases. But if we join hands and work together, we can find ways to work with people with heart problems. I also want to build a big hospital for the poor, because I love my country, Uganda.

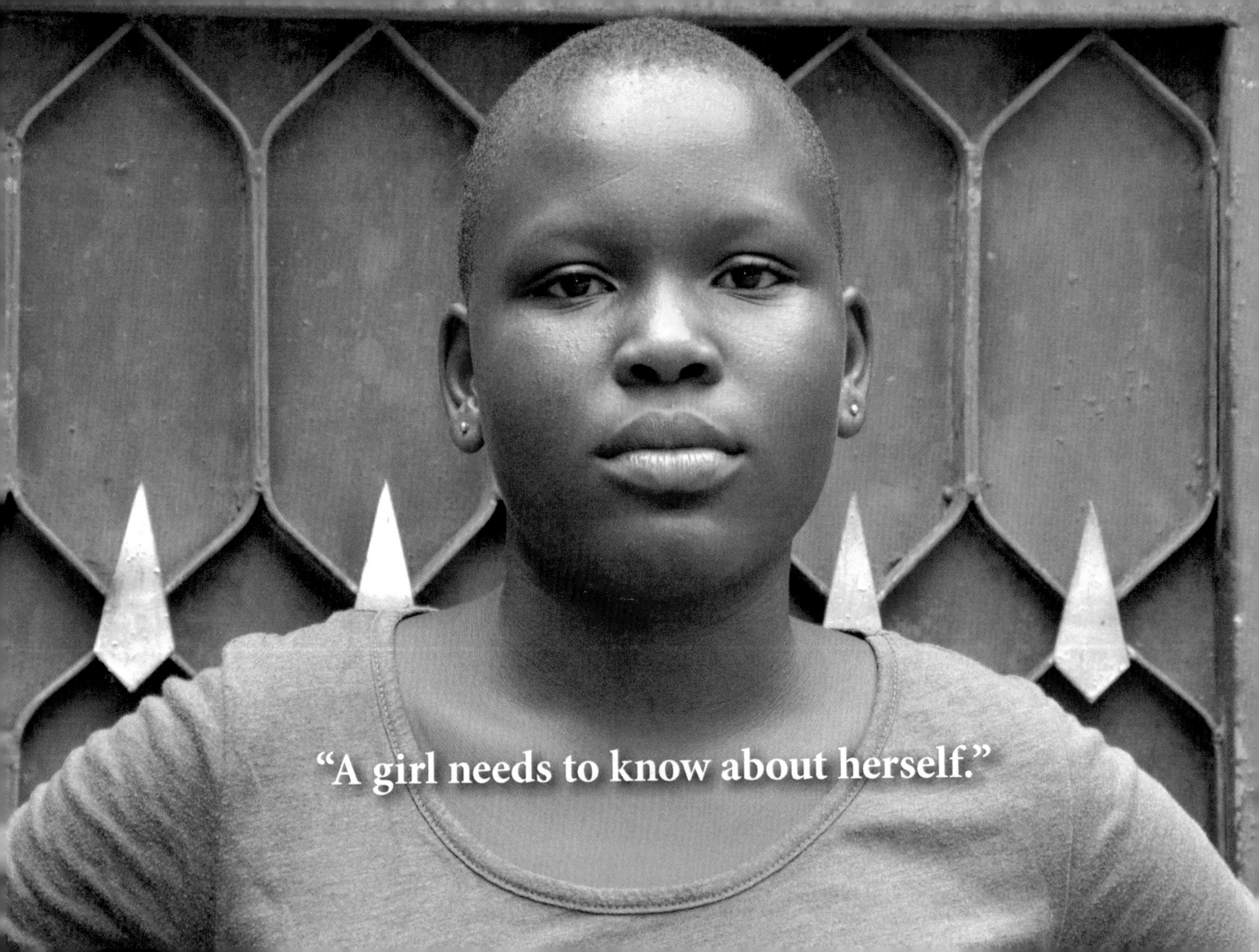
"A girl needs to know about herself."

Cherop Metrine Gloria
Age 13

Our father rejected us, so I grew up in a single-mothered family with two siblings.

My dad stays near us and we always watch him enjoying a better life with another family. We're always suffering with no food and our school fees default, causing me to be chased out of school, hence poor performance. It really hurts.

During the holidays, we used to go to the village and stay there, but, my dad went and destroyed our house leaving us homeless. I would like to give my dad another chance, but there is no way I can express it since he cannot even greet us. When we see him out in the streets, he pretends to not see us. This hurts me more.

One evening in the village, my grandparents sent me to the shop. Starting my journey back home, I looked at my left side and I saw a group of boys. I continued my journey. All the boys stood up and shouted, "You girl! You are so beautiful. You first come here."

I continued pretending to be ignorant about what was going on. I did this because of the self-esteem I developed from Girl Up Initiative Uganda. A girl was sent by these boys to come and call me. I told her that a girl needs to know about herself. I went to her home and requested to talk to her about how not to be pressured by boys' influence and about normal girls' body changes. I encouraged her to stay in school and cope with life, too. The girl is now in Secondary 3. We are still friends and the mother is proud of her.

I want other people to read my story so when a boy talks to her, they know what to do. And they know about themselves to have high self-esteem, so they can have a better future and say “NO” to boys.

I dream about being a lawyer, because many people are saying girls cannot be lawyers. I want to be a lawyer because I want to get money and help my brother by paying for school fees and food. I want to be a lawyer because I want my country to be united and be safe from law breakers.

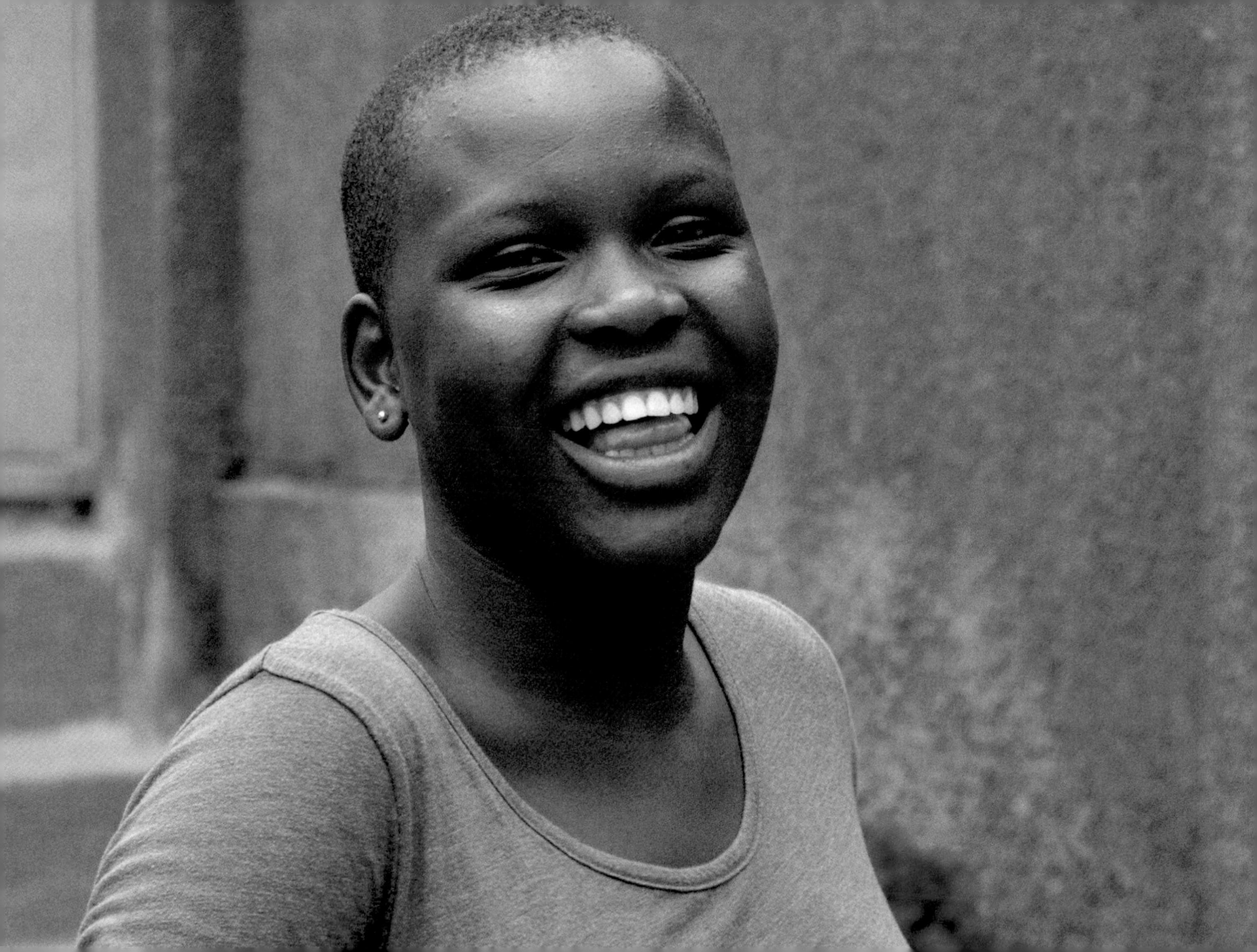

"I know that I am
not a failure.
I deserve the best."

Bashabomwe Shivan
Age 13

At home, I have four other siblings: three girls and one stepbrother. I am the last born at home. When I was in Primary 5, I became unserious about my education. I would be in class and see other children outside playing. I would be tempted to go out and play with them even when the teacher was teaching in class.

My best friend was Teddy and she liked the same things that I had started to like. She would call me to go with her outside and even spend time outside pretending to have gone to the bathroom, but we only wanted to get back to class when the lesson is ending. My performance became bad and continued to decline over time.

Very many people abused me, telling me that I am useless, hopeless, selfish, ugly, and I didn't know how to choose my friends. Because very many people told me bad words, I lost confidence. I would always think about those bad words and believe I am a failure and I am ugly. I couldn't appreciate my body and what it could do for me.

But when I got to Primary 6, we were introduced to Girl Up Initiative Uganda, and I joined. I realised that the things I had been doing were wrong and were not adding up to make school better for me. I let go of my friend who was encouraging me to play during class time and thought that it would be better to get new friends who would be helpful. My current friends are bright boys in class, and during break time, I ask them to help me with at least one math problem that I don't understand. They are not selfish, and it is because of them that my performance is becoming better again, because I do not waste a lot of time anymore.

Now, I know that I am not a failure. I deserve the best. I am confident and can talk to people who are older than me. I can choose my friends wisely. My performance in class is better. I am now among the first ten people in my class.

I can make good decisions by staying away from bad peer pressure groups and friends who do drugs and skip class, and I trust my friends who can support me that what I am doing is right.

Thank you Girl Up for helping me to become what I am today.

I am excited to share my stories because I want others to read my stories, because some girls are voiceless. I want to be the voice for those who fear, who cannot express their feelings, who are shy. I want them to be confident. I want them not to fear any person.

When a man comes and tells you that you're beautiful, you tell him, "They already told me. Every day they tell me. My mother, my father, they already tell me that I'm beautiful every day. I know that I'm beautiful."

I have lots of older boys telling me this. This makes them leave me alone. Then they become my friends.

I have a dream to become a doctor, because I want to help people in my country by treating them from the disease they are suffering from. I also want to be a doctor because doctors are respected a lot.

"I remain confident as I am."

Nanyanzi Sumayia
Age 13

Before joining Girl Up Initiative Uganda, I didn't have confidence. I feared people. It pained me a lot when I sat with a group of people and they talked about me and my color and how I was so different. So I sat alone. I didn't have any friends.

In the classroom, when our teacher asked questions and I raised my hand, the students behind me made fun of me, "What is she going to say? Funny things … that's all."

That pained me. Even in class people didn't trust me. I thought this must mean I'm nothing in this world. I cried when I went back home. I stopped raising my hand in class because of their teasing.

One day, I went with my sister to town. A group of children were playing on the path. My sister asked them to let us pass. The children said, "Who do you think you are, all special because you're with a mzungu (white-skinned person)? Because you're with a namagoya?" (The word for "albino" in the local language.)

That word pained me so much. I was annoyed, I wanted to cry, but instead, I just kept quiet. My sister asked me, "What's wrong?" But I kept saying nothing was wrong. I couldn't stand up for myself to the children, and I couldn't even tell my sister how their name-calling hurt me.

I joined Girl Up Initiative Uganda a little while later, when I was 11 years old. The coaches taught us life skills that you need to achieve your life goals and abstain from negative behaviors. When they taught us about confidence and peer pressure, I realised I could talk and speak out. I didn't need to let the teasing and peer pressure stop me.

All the girls in the club were treated the same. This helped me feel more comfortable in myself and gain more confidence. I started raising my hand and sharing answers and examples when the coaches asked us questions. I started having fun and making friends. I forgot all about the problems I used to have.

The teacher at school called together all of us girls who were in the Girl Up Club. “What happened to Sumayia?” they asked. “She’s different. She’s asking questions and talking.” They told her I was changing, and we all were changing because of Girl Up.

If people call me that word now (namagoya), I wouldn’t be annoyed. Even though they call me that, nothing change on me. I remain Sumayia. I remain who I am. Let them talk. It can’t make me die. I remain Sumayia and I remai confident as I am. It doesn’t pain me anymore. I feel happy with my color. Even now some people admire my color.

Now as a Big Sister, I get to mentor other girls. My neighbour came to me when she started her menstruation. “ have a problem. I started my menstruation, but I don’t know what to do.” She didn’t know what sanitary pads are, s I explained what they are. I told her how she could make one and use it. Now she can be clean when she starts he menstruation.

Another girl came to me in trouble. Her stepfather was going to beat her, and she didn’t want to go home. She didn have anywhere else to go. I wasn’t able to let her stay at our home, but I remembered I had one of the Girl Up coach numbers. So I called her and she coached me through what to do. I had the girl go to the Girl Up office. I gave he money for transport and told her how to get there. They were able to help her and coach her and her mom. Now the all have a better relationship.

I want to share my story so other girls know that helping others is the best gift you can give in life.

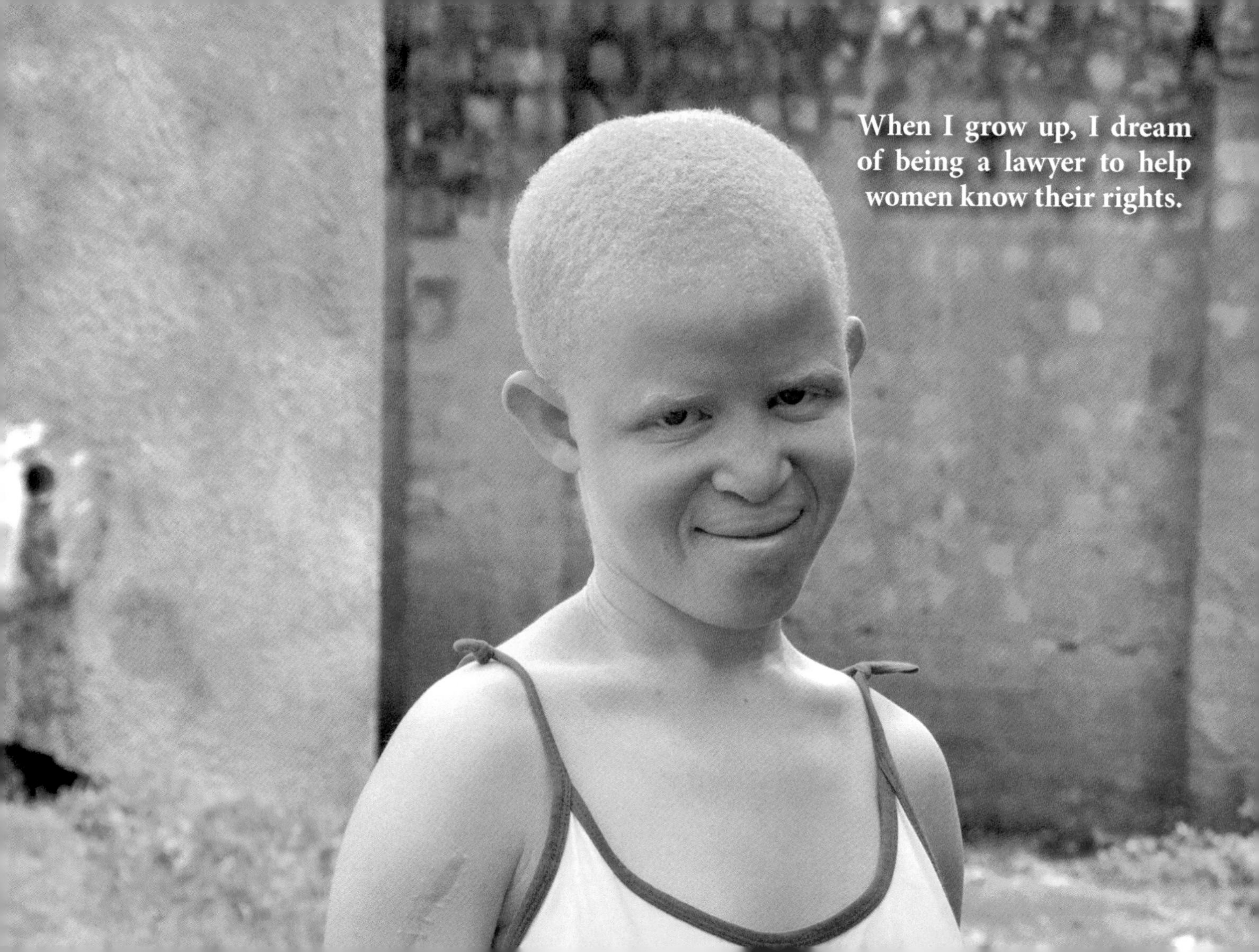

When I grow up, I dream of being a lawyer to help women know their rights.

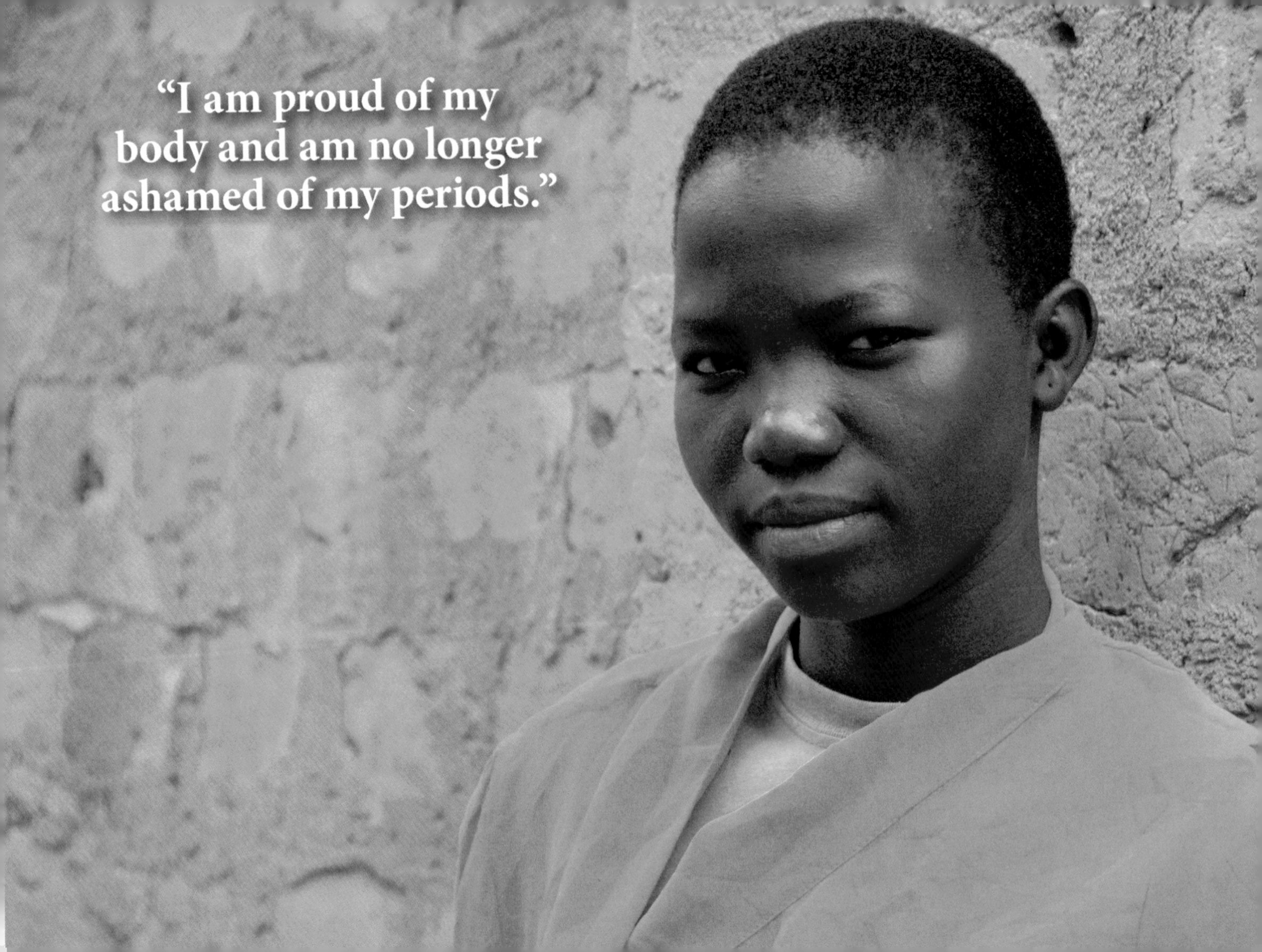
"I am proud of my body and am no longer ashamed of my periods."

Ajilong Esther
Age 13

I come from a family of six. However, I do not live with my parents. They stay in Hoima. When I was ten years old, they brought me to live with my aunt, so I could go to school in Kampala.

I used to go to school in the village, but it wasn't easy. The teachers in the village don't teach. The way they teach, it's slow because there were all different ages in the classroom.

I was very lucky when I came to Kampala. I joined Girl Up Initiative Uganda. Before Girl Up, I never knew anything about menstruation. Nobody talked about it. My sisters and friends at school would always cry during their menstruation periods because of the pain, so I was scared about how I would react when I started menstruating.

Time came, and I started my menstruation. When I noticed some blood on my skirt, I thought something had hurt me. I went back home and bathed, but remained silent without telling my aunt about the blood.

As the day passed, the blood kept on flowing, and I had no sanitary towels. I became worried. I felt bad. I cried. I didn't know what it was. I thought something was wrong with my body. My aunt saw the soiled towels and asked me about them. She bought for me pads and taught me how to use them. Now I can use them.

In the Adolescent Girls Program, they taught us that every girl gets a period. The coaches told us about body changes and how the changes are natural and normal. I was so relieved. Now I know nothing was wrong with me. I know that menstruation is for every girl and you don't need to be afraid of it. It's just a monthly thing.

They advised us to appreciate our bodies and take proper care of them, and also told us to always be confident. Since then, my confidence improved. I am proud of my body and am no longer ashamed of my periods.

The coaches also taught us how to make reusable sanitary pads. If I go to the village again, I'll teach those girls how to make them. Girls usually use banana fibers for pads or a piece of cloth.

Boys abuse girls because of menstruation. They think it means you slept with a man. Boys used to abuse me about menstruation and say things like they think I'm sleeping with someone. Or they'd say menstruation is fake. Boys have to stop what they are doing, because they do bad things.

I want other girls to read my story because I never knew anything about how my body would change, but now I know about life changes and how the body changes from here to being an adult. That helps to know that I'll go through changes, but nothing is wrong. I want other girls to know this.

I'm proud of my body. I'm proud of everything I have in my body. I'm proud that I'm a girl. Boys, they grow up and live and forget about their family. But a girl, she'll always do something to help her family be good. A girl is very responsible. I see them doing things for their families.

When I grow up, I want to become a helper and a giver just like Girl Up Initiative Uganda, because I want to help girl and teach them how to keep their bodies healthy and how their life can change for the better. I'll open a school of Gir Up and teach more girls about Girl Up.

GIRLS DARING TO DREAM

Our Dream Ceremony

We created a Dream Ceremony for a group of Big Sisters during one of their weekend programs. These girls had already participated in the year-long Adolescent Girls Program and were being trained on how to be mentors for other girls in their communities.

It's a beautiful thing, when an adolescent girl growing up in the slums has the courage to dream of a better future for herself. It's not only beautiful, it's revolutionary! In daring to dream, she's valuing herself and acknowledging her ability to change her future, regardless of her current circumstances. This is huge.

We knew that if these Big Sisters were supported in dreaming of a better future for themselves, they would be more likely to encourage their peers, sisters, cousins, and even mothers and aunts to dare to dream, too.

In the Dream Ceremony, each girl was invited to write down her dream of what she wishes to be when she grows up. Then, each girl got to read her dream out loud, and be witnessed and celebrated by a small circle of her peers and one of the coaches from the Girl Up Initiative Uganda Team. We were so inspired by these girls and their dreams that we decided to include several of them in our book so you, too, can witness them, and together, we can envision a better future for all.

"My dream is to become a musician. I want to pass my message of hope through music and reach out to the children who sleep on the streets."
Kabagweri Shifa, Age 14

"I want to become a doctor, because I want to cure HIV. I want to save lives. I want to treat parents for free."
Acen Miriam, Age 12

"I want to be an accountant, because I am a mathematician and I want other girls to know that they can do it confidently."
Kasiringi Teddy, Age 12

"I want to become like our coaches who teach other girls how to make pads, necklaces, and many other things."
Nakazibwe Shamirah, Age 12

"I want to become a staff member of Girl Up Initiative Uganda when I grow up. I want to speak for the voiceless, stop violence against girls, and fight for children's rights."
Ajambo Vanessa, Age 10

"I want to become a pilot. I want to fly in every country and continent. And I also want to challenge all those people who thought that girls cannot fly aeroplanes. That's not true, because all people in the world can achieve their goals. I believe in myself that I can make it and I can achieve my dream. I am proud of who I am."
Pimer Prossy, Age 12

"I want to be a nurse and help mothers in the hospital during labor time."
Awori Rebecca, Age 13

"I want to be a tourist, so that I can move to different countries to know more about them."
Ainomugisha Desire, Age 10

"When I grow up, I will become a queen dancer. I will become a celeb. In my dream, I want to help my parents when I become a celeb."
Ngabire Shadia, Age 10

"I want to be a lawyer, because I want to help people who cannot speak out for themselves."
Atenyo Tracy, Age 11

"I want to become a doctor, because I want to challenge the saying that women are meant for kitchen responsibilities only."
Adongo Pauline, Age 13

"When I grow up, I want to be a teacher, so that I give children a good future."
Komuntale Pearl, Age 9

"My dream is to become a midwife. I want to be a doctor to challenge people that girls can even be doctors. I want to trea pregnant mothers who die in hospitals. I want to have a good life and to treat my parents and relatives."
Letasi Fiona, Age 11

"I want to be a dancer, because it is my talent and I am proud of it."
Kusassira Vanessa, Age 12

"I want to become a pilot, because I don't want my parents to hav paid school fees for nothing. I want to show my parents that I wa not eating money which they have been giving me for school fees In our family, many people don't like to be pilots. I want to take m parents out in my aeroplane."
Akandinda Prize, Age 12

"I want to become a bank manager, because banks need people to work in them. Not only men work in banks, women do, also. In the future, I also want to build an orphanage to help orphans who do not have someone to help them, so they can have a better life."
Mutesi Elizabeth, Age 13

"I want to become a lawyer. I want to promote justice in the country."
Ainembabazi Lucky, Age 14

"I want to become a musician in the future, because music makes me happy. Whenever I am sad, I sing a song and I cool down. I want to make people happy, become famous, help the needy, have fun, and empower other people to also never give up through the songs I will be singing."
Ayugi Claire, Age 12

"I want to become a barber, because I want to plate people's hair so that they will look nice."
Apio Josephine, Age 11

"I want to become a surgeon because in a country like Uganda, there are very few doctors who operate on sick people. I want to help people who are in need."
Atiang Patience, Age 13

THE 5 BIGGEST BARRIERS THAT KEEP GIRLS IN UGANDA FROM ACCESSING A QUALITY EDUCATION

Barrier #1: Poverty

As Seen Through The Coaches' Eyes:

- Families with four to eight or more children sometime share a single-room home.
- There is no electricity.
- There is poor sanitation: no clean water and no drainage.
- When it rains, trenches filled with dirty water, urine, and feces, that run throughout the slums, overflow, entering people's homes.
- There is a high crime rate.
- Most families don't have money for healthcare.
- Disease and sickness are rampant.
- Even if they're able to go to school, girls often don't have books or supplies.
- Girls usually own one dress and undergarment that they wash without soap, because families can't afford it.
- Everyone struggles for food. It is common for girls to receive only one meal per day like posho: a stiff, dough-like dish made from ground maize.

How Girl Up Initiative Uganda Works To Overcome Poverty:

In recognition of the challenges facing girls growing up in extreme poverty, Girl Up Initiative Uganda has designe all its programs to include an element of entrepreneurship and business skills development. In the Adolescent Girl Program, the girls receive hands-on skills development and training, learning how to make bags, mats, jewelr briquettes, and reusable sanitary pads for personal use and/or to sell. GUIU also offers school scholarships to suppor girls in finishing their primary education.

GUIU has another program, the Young Women's Economic Empowerment Program, which teaches young wome vocational skills, increases their entrepreneurial knowledge, and provides them with employment opportunities.

In addition, GUIU believes in offering employment and volunteer opportunities for young women from the sam urban slum communities as its program participants. In this way, GUIU helps poor communities by providin employment opportunities for local youth while also allowing the organization to better understand the experienc of program participants.

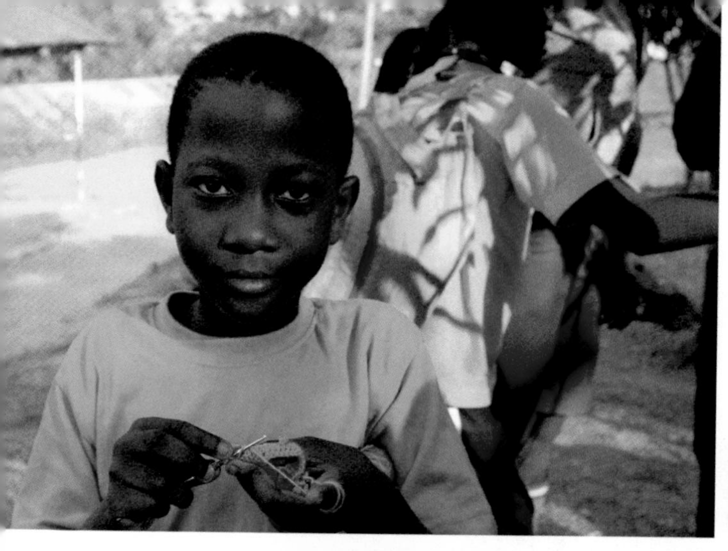

Barrier #2: Gender-Based Violence/Sexual Abuse

As Seen Through The Coaches' Eyes:

- Girls, especially those growing up in the slums, are not respected. As they walk along the road, men whistle at them, touch their breasts, and call them names.
- Girls are viewed as sex objects that can be used any time the user feels like it. Their rights are violated constantly. This positions men as superior to girls/women. Consequently, girls have low self-esteem and low confidence.
- Girls don't know their rights. They don't know that this violence is considered illegal. It's just the "way of life" they've become accustomed to.
- Girls constantly have to protect themselves against gender-based violence, pressure for early sex, and pregnancy.

How Girl Up Initiative Uganda Works To Overcome Gender-Based Violence/Sexual Abuse:

GUIU helps girls overcome this barrier by working at both the individual and collective level. In the Adolescent Girls Program, the girls are taught about their rights according to national and international law. The AGP places emphasis on gender-based violence and how to speak up against it. Girls are taught how to communicate assertively, and to regularly practice using their voices.

The team also accompanies the girls on field trips to the local Child Protection Unit and to the Girl Up Office, so they know where to go to report cases of violence. In such cases, the Girl Up coaches mediate a solution with the parents or guardians to find a way forward. The organization has since seen an increase in the number of girls reporting cases of violence.

GUIU also recognizes that it is essential to work with the community to end gender-based violence and create safe environments for girls. The organization works closely with local leaders in Kampala (including religious and political leaders, police, youth leaders, health facilities, school administrators and teachers, and parents/guardians) to transform deeply held beliefs around gender inequality, and to prevent and protect against gender-based violence. This approach strengthens existing community structures and places value on collaboration, involving more community members in ending gender-based violence, thereby giving even more legitimacy to the issue.

Violence Against Girls.
Gender Based Violence
Violence?
SCENARIOS
Paul likes Martha, he gives her gifts to have sex with her. Paul does not use force.
1 Physical Violence
2 Sexual Violence
for example.
Rape
Defilement
Sexual Harrasment

Barrier #3: Lack Of Girl-Friendly School Environments

As Seen Through The Coaches' Eyes:

- Adolescent girls are bullied by boys during their menstrual cycles.
- Some girls face sexual harassment and abuse by male teachers. One girl explained that a male teacher often touched her, buttoning and unbuttoning her shirt. Others demand sex for good grades.
- In the schools, there is no comprehensive sex education. Students only learn about sex in biology classes.
- Some teachers believe that boys are more intelligent than girls, and therefore pay more attention to the boys.
- Adolescent girls are often told they are studying for nothing due to stereotypes that say girls are assets who are only there to produce, cook, and take care of the home; they are demotivated to attend school as it is reiterated that only men are suited for various professions.

How Girl Up Initiative Uganda Works To Overcome Lack Of Girl-Friendly Schoo Environments:

GUIU ensures that each school where the AGP is present provides a girl-friendly environment by establishing "talkin compounds": signs are placed throughout the schoolyards that deliver messages such as "Books Before Babies," an "Speak Out Against Violence."

The GUIU team includes school administrators and teachers in their trainings so they receive the same knowledge an skills the girls do. This empowers them to support girls in their schools even more.

Girl Up girls are trained to be leaders in their schools to ensure a friendly environment for all girls. They are supporte to lead advocacy activities in their communities like trash cleanups and awareness campaigns. They're also encourage to perform short theatre pieces during school assemblies to raise awareness about the issues they face at school and home.

The AGP educates girls on puberty, menstruation, and their changing bodies. Girls are given the opportunity t discuss and ask questions freely, which begins to break the stigma and myths around menstruation. The girls als learn how to make their own reusable sanitary pads. This prevents them from missing school during menstruation an teaches them a valuable income-generating skill.

Girl Up
Initiative Uganda
BOOKS
BEFORE
BABIES

Girls And Menstruation

One of the girls in the AGP, Ajilong Esther, wrote this poem that reflects how menstruation is beginning to be accepted and even embraced by these adolescent girls.

~ Menstruation ~

Menstruation Menstruation
How I imagine if you were not there for me
Many girls in Uganda are crying because of you
Missing school because of you, fearing to be open because of you
And how I wish you could tell us the day you will come
Many girls are lacking what to use and even pads during their period.

May you stay longer because we still need you in our lives
Without you, our mothers could not produce children,
Marriage and other thing and I really thank God because
He has given me a wonderful period.

Girls, women, let us come together to solve this problem.

Therefore, we say menstruation is needed in our lives
So we can be free, menstruation doesn't kill but help us
And it teaches us how to care for our bodies as girls.

Barrier #4: Early Marriage And Teenage Pregnancy

As Seen Through The Coaches' Eyes:

- There is a lot of pressure on girls to trade sex for food or money for their family.
- Many girls think their only option in life is to get married and have children.
- Girls are seen as assets—valued for the bride price the family will receive for the marriage.
- Girls are expected to get married, have children, and work hard to please their husband.
- If a girl gets pregnant while in school, the school rarely (if ever) allows her back in while she is pregnant or after giving birth. She is shamed, whereas the boy or man who got her pregnant can continue his life as normal.
- Many men are resistant to using condoms, thereby leading to increasing rates of HIV, especially among young women who are not empowered to demand condom use.
- It is almost impossible for girls to access contraception at local health facilities, because the nurses and doctors will not see them if they don't come with a man.
- Family planning is still resisted as it is seen as a Western intervention to reduce the African population.

How Girl Up Initiative Uganda Works To Overcome Early Marriage And Teenage Pregnancy:

The AGP educates girls on their sexual and reproductive health and rights, while building their confidence, self-esteem, and feelings of self-worth. This empowers them to resist negative peer pressure and stand up for their rights GUIU also organizes sexual and reproductive health mobile clinics so young women and girls can access free youth friendly services.

Girls are taught how to assertively say "NO" to unwanted sexual attention. They learn that there are consequences fo all of their actions and are encouraged to stay in school and focus on their dreams, rather than on having boyfriends They are also taught about national and international laws around child marriage, so they can report any cases of chil marriage in their own lives, or in the lives of their friends and family.

The AGP also places an emphasis on self-awareness via identifying strengths. This allows girls to learn to love themselve no matter what others do to them, and to accept and understand others. For instance, the girls have told us how the have supported friends who got pregnant at a young age while others were shaming and discriminating against them

GUIU also has young women lead the programs, which positions them as role models for the girls. All of the GUIU coaches are from the same slum communities as the girls, and are either college graduates, or still attending universit Having these coaches as positive role models gives the girls hope and instills the belief that they too can escape th cycle of poverty and gender inequality and do something more with their lives.

PLAN
Girl Up
Girl Up

Barrier #5: Gender Inequality

As Seen Through the Coaches' Eyes:

- There is a widely believed myth that males are stronger and more important than females. Girls are viewed as inferior, less sensible and weaker than boys.
- Boys are given more time to study and play. Girls are expected to stay home, do housework, cook and care for younger siblings.
- Men speak freely and make all the decisions in the home. Women are not allowed to participate in family or community meetings.
- Girls are taught that making eye contact and asking questions is rude and disrespectful. They are expected to be submissive and do what they are told.
- When they do speak, girls are expected to talk softly and calmly.
- Girls learn that what they think and feel doesn't matter, and not worthy of expressing.
- Girls are not taught to make decisions for themselves. They are expected to do what they're told; thus, they're easily influenced by others and can get involved with bad peer groups.
- Girls are reluctant to dream, because all they see around them are women and girls being treated like second-class citizens who have no voice and choice in their own lives.

How Girl Up Initiative Uganda Works To Overcome Gender Inequality:

GUIU works to ensure that girls are recognized as active agents of change in their schools and communities. By empowering girls individually and collectively to challenge the patriarchal social order, they become spokespersons for girls' rights and drivers of systemic change in the community.

The AGP focuses on building girls' capacities in community outreach and advocacy, so they can express their idea freely in public spaces. Advocacy initiatives include forum theatre outreach performances, marches, and othe awareness programs around girls' education and rights.

The overarching goal of Girl Up Initiative Uganda is to shift gender imbalances so that women are provided the sam rights, opportunities, and respect as men. The organization recognizes that education and economic empowermer programs are key to breaking down the barriers that propagate poverty and gender inequality.

When girls and women have access to an education, they are more likely to earn an income, have fewer children an healthier families, send their children to school, and contribute to the development of their communities. They ar also less likely to experience domestic violence.

This is why GUIU works closely with local leaders to bring awareness to the importance of girls' education and gend equality. By building up existing reputable local structures, GUIU ensures that community leaders are valued partners who have a stake in ensuring that girls and women receive equal educational and employment opportunitie The organization invites all partners to community events to join the cause and stand up for girls' rights.

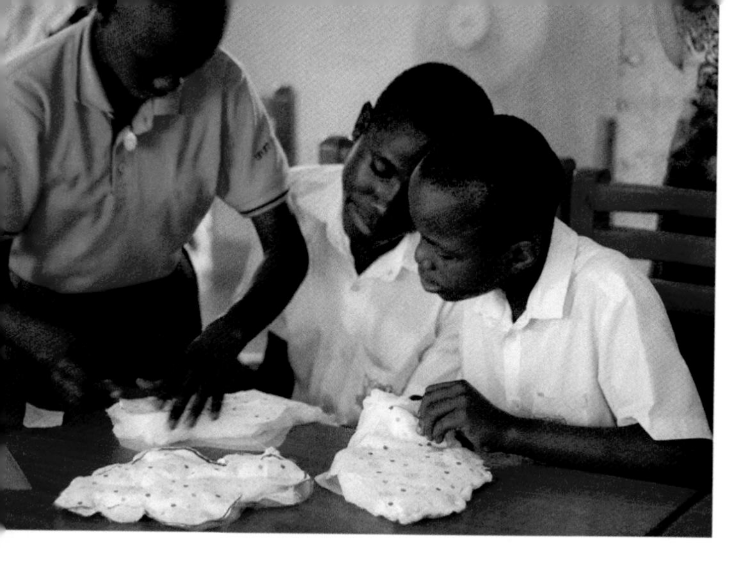

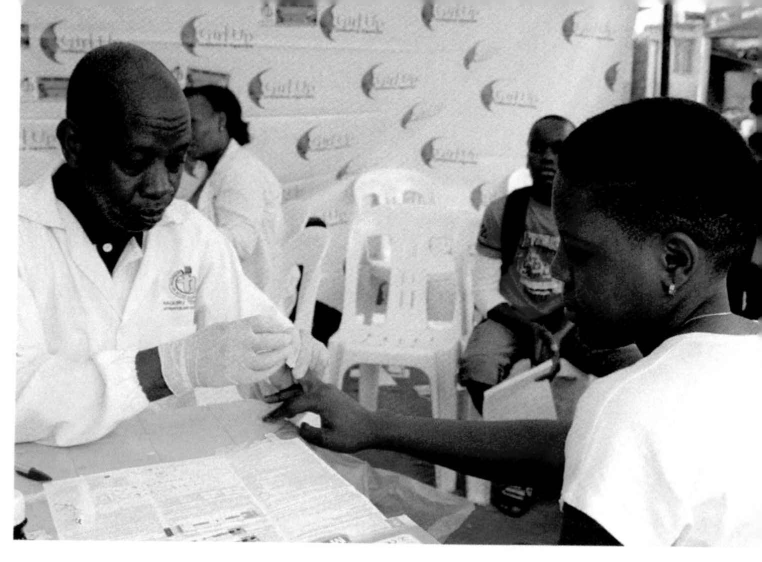

TOGETHER WE CAN
STOP VIOLENCE
AGAINST GIRLS
BE MEDIA
LITERATES
AND CRITIAL
ASPIRE TO INSPIRE
REMEMBER
VIOLENCE
IS A CHOIC
I AM
PROUD TO BE
AGIRL
STOP
STREET
HARRASMEN
NEVER BE
ASHAMED

HOW TO GET INVOLVED

Girl Up
Girl Up

Thank you for contributing to the well-being of the adolescent girls featured in this book, and the other girls in the Adolescent Girls Program, through your donation to our book. We truly appreciate your generosity.

We also know that by now, you may be wondering how you can stay connected, and perhaps even get more involved, either with Girl Up Initiative Uganda, or other great organizations that are empowering girls around the world.

Get Connected on Social Media

Facebook: **facebook.com/girlupuganda**

Twitter: **twitter.comk/GirlUpUganda**

Instagram: **instagram.com/GirlUpUganda**

Subscribe to the Girl Up Uganda YouTube Channel.

Sign up for our newsletter on our website here: **girlupuganda.org**

Once you get connected, please stay connected! When you comment on and/or share our posts, you help us raise awareness about our transformative work and inspire others to join our movement of positive change.

Volunteer

Interested in volunteering your time, energy, and special skills to our organization, either in person or virtually? If so, please contact us at: info@girlupuganda.org to learn more.

Donate

As a non-profit organization, donations are a vital source of our funding. We rely on the generosity of donors like you to run our programs and contribute to our girls and communities in impactful ways. You can donate with a one time payment, or you can make a monthly donation. While any amount is greatly appreciated, here is an idea of how specific amounts are invested:

- $75: Covers one girl's school fees for one year.
- $100: Provides 20 girls with materials to make a pack of reusable sanitary pads.
- $250: Enables four girls to join the AGP year-long training program.
- $1000: Funds the salary for one junior/trainee seamstress at Mazuri Designs for one year.
- $3000: Covers medical insurance for all staff members for one year.

To donate, please visit: **www.girlupuganda.org/donate**

Share Our Book

Interested in getting additional copies of our book to share with your family, friends, local school, and community? You can find us on Amazon!

Help Us Get The Word Out

One of our goals is to raise awareness and reach more people around the world with our message of empowering girls. Our message is global; girls all around the world face issues similar to those described in this book.

Do you know anyone who hosts a radio show, podcast, or other virtual platform who might be interested in interviewing one or both of the Co-Founders about the great work they're doing in Girl Up Initiative Uganda? If so, please contact us with details: info@girlupuganda.org

Get Connected and Involved Locally

Girl Up Initiative Uganda's programs are based in Uganda, and therefore, it may be a bit challenging for you to provide face-to-face support.

That's why we're sharing the following United States-based organizations, which might be a bit easier for you to become involved in:

Girls Inc.: girlsinc.org
Big Brothers Big Sisters of America: bbs.org
Boys and Girls Clubs of America: bgca.org
Young Women's Christian Association: ywca.org
Court Appointed Special Advocates for Children: casaforchildren.org
National Foster Parent Association: nfpaonline.org

Inspire and Empower Locally

In general, adolescent girls don't feel seen and heard, and they crave both. They have so many feelings and thought swirling inside as their bodies, hormones, and interests change.

Listening is the single best thing you can do to build rapport and open conversation with an adolescent girl. Tha doesn't mean agreeing with what they are saying. It just means that you care to know what they think and feel abou whatever is of interest to them.

Here are a few easy, powerful, and tangible ways you can support and mentor the girls in your own family, neighborhoo and community:

1. Invite her to tell you about herself.
2. Ask her about her hopes and dreams.
3. Encourage her to share the details of her day with you.
4. Invite her to write a list of her strengths and what she likes about herself: words of acknowledgment that can keep her encouraged and believing in herself. (This is an exercise that the AGP Coaches complete with their girls.)

Listen to whatever she shares without judgment, interpretation, or interruption. You don't need to try to fix anythin Instead, support her in finding her own way.

ACKNOWLEDGEMENTS

We are grateful to the Girl Up Initiative Uganda Book Dream Team for contributing their time, talents, care, coordination, and love to this project, every step of the way.

Gloria Komukama and Marion Achom: Thank you for the endless hours you contributed to scheduling logistics and facilitating 1:1 conversations with the girls so we could capture their stories. We also appreciate your prayers, ongoing positivity, and willingness to do what it took to turn our book idea into a reality. And truly, it is your dedication to these girls, and your mentorship, that has catalyzed their transformation. Thank you for being allies and advocates for the thousands of girls growing up in Kampala. Your day-to-day involvement with these girls is making a positive difference on the planet, and for this we are eternally grateful.

Emmanuel Walusimbi: You have captured the beauty, strength, intensity, and essence of each of the girls featured in our book. Their powerful words, partnered with your potent images, create even more compelling stories. We appreciate the many hours you logged in for the photoshoots with the girls and around Kampala. Thank you for sharing your gift of photography with us!

Kimberly Wolf: Thank you for your immediate and unwavering support of our book, from the very inception of the idea to its final steps of completion and beyond. Your editing, feedback, encouragement, vision, and commitment to this book, and the girls in the GUIU programs and beyond, is priceless!

Monica Nyiraguhabwa: Thank you for your dedication to creating a city, country, and ultimately a world where girls have a choice and a voice in everything that involves and impacts them. Your vision, strength, and fortitude to never give up, and to overcome the obstacles of poverty and inequality that you faced, have contributed to the successful existence of Girl Up Initiative Uganda, and the thousands of girls touched by your programs. These girls would not have these stories of transformation to share had it not been for your own transformation and desire to pay it forward. Thank you, beyond words.

We also wish to thank all the other **Girl Up Initiative Uganda Coaches** who contributed so much to our book! They supported the writing workshops and Dream Ceremony we did with the girls, as well as shared their insights and stories of what it's really like for adolescent girls growing up in the slums of Kampala (that information was used to write "The Five Biggest Barriers That Keep Girls In Uganda From Accessing A Quality Education" section of our book). You all are AMAZING, and we love you like CRAZY!

Caroline Achola
Saidi Alikwan
Joan Atimango
Miriam Kabayo
Enock Kyambadde
Annet Kyokutamba
Hajara Namuyimbwa
Clare Natukunda
Sharon Nayebare
Michael Oonyu
Ivan Kenneth Opio
Jane Tushabe
Clare Tusingwire
Allan Denis Zziwa

We were very fortunate to have an advocate and "Book Angel" in the form of **Connie Viveros** and **The Inspired Hear Foundation**. Thank you, Connie, for believing in our project, and believing in us. Your spiritual guidance couple with your pragmatic, nitty-gritty wisdom, design acumen, and support were essential to making this book a success You have a special gift for fueling creative projects inspired by the soul!

We also wish to give thanks to the three women who reviewed our manuscript and provided essential feedbac before it was sent to the publisher: **Missy Singer-Dumars, Barbara Carroll**, and **Susyn Reeve.** Thank you for you contribution to getting our book to where it is now.

We are overflowing with gratitude for our publisher, **Love-Based Publishing**. Thank you, **Paul Wacek**, for you dedication to designing our book to match our vision. Thank you, **Megan Yakovich**, for being our eagle eyes an expert editor. Thank you, **Michele PW**, for taking on our unique project and appreciating how grief can be a catalys for creation.

THANK YOU TO OUR DONORS!

A HUGE THANK YOU to the generous people who contributed over $6,000 to our fundraiser. They made it possible for us to get our book published, printed, and in your hands right now!

Special acknowledgment goes to the following donors who donated $100 USD or more:

Amy Arszman Daso, MD
Amy, Nylah & Mike Hudgens
Anne Dixon
Bill, Kristen, Nathan & Molly Potter
Christel Joy Crawford
Clifford Meurer
Cory Michelle
Dr. Lisa Cooney
Ginny Jordan
Jennifer D. Walrod
Jill, Russell & Sophia Cohn
Joan Rothaus
Julie Romero & Family
Katie, Chris, Emma & Melanie Brandt
Kendra E Thornbury
Kim Sheeran Zoller
Lea Black & Laura Faux-Donnelly
Lisa Bendt
Lou & Connie Viveros
Maria Fynn
Mary Wong
Melanie Munir
Nate, Tara, Ashlee & Adalyn Walrod
Robyn M James
Rod Rothaus
Shalini Joshi Yamdagni
Tamra Fleming
The Speek Family
Trevor Hallenbeck

We appreciate your generosity of spirit and could not have done this without you! Mwebale nyo!

ABOUT GIRL UP INITIATIVE UGANDA

CORE

Girl Up Initiative Uganda (GUIU) is a non-profit organization located in Kampala, Uganda, that provides comprehensive education and economic empowerment programs for adolescent girls and young women, so they can thrive as leaders in their communities. Girls gain crucial information about their human rights, puberty, peer pressure, the prevention of gender-based violence, and much more. They also learn hands-on practical skills like making reusable sanitary pads, so that they do not miss school during their menstrual periods.

GUIU recognizes that education, specifically a holistic life-skills training program, and economic empowerment programs are key to unlocking the barriers of poverty and gender inequality. When the overall wellbeing of girls is put at the forefront of development interventions, a girl understands the importance of gaining control over her life and body. She develops her confidence and begins to speak up against violence. This lowers her chance of falling into the major challenges faced by girls in Uganda: child marriage, sexual violence, exposure to HIV/AIDS, and teenage pregnancy.

Since 2013, the Adolescent Girls Program (AGP) has been delivered in nine government-funded schools and has directly impacted over 1,475 girls. When the girls graduate from the AGP, they can join the Big Sisters Network to receive additional leadership training and support, so they can serve as mentors to other girls. Through our post-training evaluations, we've discovered that all the girls have passed on their knowledge and skills to others in the community: 92% to close friends and 8% to others (mothers, aunts, cousins, peers, etc.). This illustrates the larger, positive "ripple effect" of this program, and how our training reaches far beyond the individual girls that are trained. Girls are eager to share their knowledge in support of uplifting and empowering others.

The Dream Team! From left to right, sitting: Sayid, Monica, Kim. Second row: Annet, Miriam, Clare, Jane, Gloria, Claire. Back row: Emma, Enock, Sharon, Joan, Ivan, Megan, Carol, Allan Denis. (Not all team members reflected in this image.)

ABOUT MEGAN WALROD

Girl Up
Girl Up

Megan Walrod, Founder of Live Your Yes, LLC, is an author, speaker, humanitarian, and heart-based copywriter and business coach. She encourages her clients to "Live Your Yes," knowing that when we live an inspired life, we are more magnetic and create greater success for everyone. Over the past decade, she has helped hundreds of women entrepreneurs build profitable and purposeful businesses. She has supported clients in successful six- and seven-figure launches, and written copy for million-dollar global business owners and non-profits.

Recently, Megan spent six months "Living Her Yes" in Uganda. Following her deep desire to pay her privilege forward, she volunteered with Girl Up Initiative Uganda. "We Have Something to Say" is a powerful expression of her calling and commitment to empower women and girls to find their voice, claim their value, and share their gifts with the world.